Joseph Alexander was born in the West Midlands of England. In his early days he was educated in secondary modern schools. He went on to college and university.

From the age of four, he saw what he could only explain at the time as people who were not there.

His whole life has been spent in the service of uniting the spirit world with the human world.

He is a man full of compassion, and all his works are written with great humour and fun. He says that there is nothing mystical or special about himself. Each one of us, as a child of God, has the ability to have the same connections with the unseen world. His famous saying is that "God does not dismiss us, it is we who dismiss God". He says that God is there for the believer and the unbeliever, for the good and the bad, because God's love is unconditional.

The author is a happy, uncomplicated man, who is never happier than when walking the dog and writing books.

By the same author

The Mystical Life of Christ
My Life Between Two Worlds

Talking with Spirit

JOSEPH ALEXANDER

Dunollie

First published in 2004 by
Dunollie Limited

UK Distribution Agent:
Crandon Press
PO Box 300
Wells-next-the-Sea
Norfolk
NR23 1WP

www.josephalexander.net

Printed and bound in Great Britain by Biddles Ltd, King's Lynn

ISBN 0 9548526 0 5

Dedicated
to Daniel Sanderson
and to Struan McDougall
for all their kindness
and hard work
in bringing
this book
together

Contents

Introduction

I was born into an ordinary family, inasmuch as I lived in a house with my mother and my brothers and sisters. Mother divorced my father when I was still very young. She then set about feeding us small ones and somewhat ministering to our needs, with the words "I want" never falling far from her ears.

In my early years I was a bit of a nuisance to my family, constantly twittering things like, "Mum, why do I keep seeing these strange things? What are these people doing here? They talk really funny. And they're wearing silly clothes…"

By the time I was twenty, I understood much more about my strange visitations. Oh yes, I knew it all by then. I was a man of the world, with special powers. I was a knight in shining armour. My dream was to charge through the world putting wrongs to right, and rescuing all the damsels, whether they wanted to be rescued or not. Of course I was as green as the salads I have these days for lunch, and just as limp, I might add.

You would think that working with Spirit would make life easier, and I agree that in some ways it has, but more than anything it brings responsibilities – ones that frequently take over your personal life. You are responsible for whatever comes out of your mouth in the name of Spirit, and you are always mindful of that. And certainly people look at you in a different light. Because you are dealing with knowledge and understanding from another world, inevitably they see you as some kind of guru or mystic, and think you must have an halo tucked away somewhere in your pocket. All this is complete nonsense. I am human with human frailties, like all of us. Nonetheless, I am aware that working with Spirit has made me try harder to reach certain goals. Emotionally there has been plenty of gruel over the years, although there have been chocolate cakes and jam sandwiches thrown in, too.

One thing I'm sure I'll never stop wondering about is why this life with Spirit came to me. I have my own theories about it, but that's all they are – theories.

I am often asked if I am a religious man. But the simple and accurate answer to that is, "No, I am not."

I have an abiding and total faith in God, and the existence of a spirit world is a matter of day-to-day experience for me. My perceptions of spirituality are as old as mankind, and as new as the time I live in.

My aim in writing this book is simply to set out how my life and my experiences have been. It is not my intention to try to convert anyone to my way of thinking. Each of us has our own road to follow. It is my wish to make a different viewpoint available in a multi-faceted world, as other people's perceptions can enrich our own lives and give us cause for reflection on a wide variety of ideas. My own life has been enriched beyond recognition by those I have had the pleasure to work with, who come both from this world and the next.

Now in my dotage I sit here with a shiny new computer in front of me, a coffee pot beside me, a personal assistant who does lots of clever things, and a book company that treats me like I'm the best thing since sliced bread. Life has become smoother and easier now, and still nothing can take away the joy I feel when I look back at my notes and think about everything that has happened in my work with Spirit.

And now I know how those people who win the Oscars feel, standing there trying to remember all the people who have helped them in their lives.

Thank you, everyone who has helped make me what I am today. Thank you, my guides, you have had great patience with me. And still do.

Titus Speaks His Truth

It is written in the Great Book of Life: "In the beginning God created heaven and earth. And the earth was without form, and void; and darkness was upon the face of the deep."

Well, my understanding is that in the beginning there was no earth, so there was no darkness or void – in the beginning there was only heaven.

The greatest minds since the beginning of time have questioned how the physical universe began, and I do not try to match the giddy heights of their brainpower. My intellect is simple. But the people of the divine world whom I deal with leave me gasping for breath at the power of their reasoning, such is their intelligence. So why, I ask, did they choose to work with me!? Who knows, but maybe the answer is that the simpler a person's mind is, the easier it is to reach..?

Whatever their reason may be, my simplicity has helped me. By listening, and learning the law of God's will, I have developed into an integrated human being, aware of the spirit within me. I have understood that we are all lent by God to further the development of our souls by being a part of the world of creation. I have learned that we are responsible for ourselves, but that we also have the responsibility of caring for each other, in whatever situation we may find ourselves.

God allows mankind to understand all that there is to know about the human experience, and about the deep spiritual side of the soul. This is a fact, and I state it with assurance.

The greatest truth I have ever learned in my life is that God reaches out to each and every one of us, according to our personal and individual development. This is the case whether we are talking about a good soul or a dark soul – God's love is equal for all. In other words, God's love is unconditional – unlike the human experience, where love expects something in return.

Everyone who follows the Christian teachings, or those of any reasoning faith, knows that God sends great souls to show us how to live our lives in this world, and to help us prepare for the next. I am always amazed at the readiness of God to forgive each and every in-

discretion, and to reward our goodness with the same grace. Oh! If only mankind could work along the same lines! Don't think that God doesn't chastise us, for he certainly does. What loving mother would not point out the error of her children's ways? What loving father would not show his children the right thing to do? Like human parents, God does not and will not condone wrong behaviour, but like us as parents, he still loves us and will guide us to the right road. I do so love the saying "And he sends his angels to take charge over you."

Over the years I have read the books and listened to the words of the greatest thinkers of our times, yet they rarely agree, even on a single question. And how can they? We are all individuals. That is how God meant us to be, of course.

Collectively, there are souls who think along similar lines as each other. They unite under the banner of one of the many religions. Each religion maintains that it is right.

The guides say that **God** *is right, and that faith in God, and faith in the personal relationship between God and each individual soul is what counts. Listening to human beings and their interpretations has its pitfalls. Certainly we must all be tolerant of each other's views. But above all it is God's laws we must trust in.*

Titus: When will you be finished waffling so we can get on with writing this book?

Joseph: Soon.

Titus: Well, then..?

Joseph: I've got quite a few questions to ask.

Titus: Well ask them, then.

Joseph: OK, well, could you tell me, is there any such thing as a demon that we refer to as the devil, and is it the embodiment of pure evil?

Titus: Yes.

Joseph: Does this demon have dominion over the world?

Titus: Only to the extent that people give power to it. People make their choices.

Joseph: Could you explain what you mean a bit more?

Titus: As people pay homage to the goodness of God, they recognise within themselves their need to relate their fears, to express their innermost secrets to a power far beyond mortal beings, to trust a power with their very souls.

Joseph: But why was so evil a presence allowed into the world of humans?

Titus: That would take far more explaining than this book could hold, but knowing how determined you are to learn, I shall attempt to give you an answer. This presence came into existence long before the world of mankind. The demon, in the beginning, was a very beautiful angel and reigned with God in perfect peace and harmony.

Joseph: Excuse me, Titus, but how was it that God, being all-powerful, did not know how this presence would react to his power?

Titus: Do you mind! Kindly let me finish my answer before you come charging in like a bull in a china shop!

I consider myself severely chastised.

Titus: The time came when the angel decided that it would like to be the all-powerful spirit. But with this decision, it became the fallen angel. There was no room for such conflict in heaven, nor, frankly, for such pretence. So God, being the deity, and full of love, cast the fallen one out from his presence. The energy released on that day was immense beyond any human conception. It is this energy, commonly known as the Big Bang, that began the physical universe. Remember, Joseph, this is a very simplified overview.

Joseph: Did God really make the world in seven days? We know heaven was already there, but what about the physical universe?

Titus: The elements that go to make up the universe came about in a millionth of a second. The rest, as you well know, happened over the course of time.

Joseph: So the world was not made in seven days, as we are told it was?

Titus: Joseph, what have I just said to you?!! Do you not listen to what I say?

Joseph: Sorry, Titus, but what I meant to ask was this: Was the whole plan for the universe implemented in the timescale described in the Good Book?

Titus: No. Science knows that things of every nature took time to develop. Time is irrelevant to God.

Joseph: So God intended for prehistoric animals and early man to develop in the way they did?

Titus: Yes, of course. This has brought a richness of life to you and to all people. It has brought much for you to learn, understand, and marvel at.

Joseph: Are we at the stage of creation that God meant us to be at?

Titus: My oh my oh my! Do you think you are?

Joseph: Well, it's hard for me to tell. Sometimes I feel we are. Then we go and do stupid things like warring with each other. Or our leaders do appalling things that affect the poor and the helpless in our society. So thinking about it, no, I don't believe we are where God wants us to be.

Titus: The human race has made many advances, but it is still in its infancy as far as its spirituality is concerned.

Joseph: Dare I ask you a question, Titus, about how God sees us, and how far up the ladder of progress we are?

Titus: God sees you all as individuals. God sees you in the way a father sees each of his children – as personalities in their own right.

Joseph: I know that is so very true, of course, Titus. How does God see nations?

Titus: God sends to mankind, through the enlightened ones, his messages of how he wishes you to proceed with the human race. You will know from human history that God has spoken to you right throughout the ages. All the Good Books of all the nations talk of God sending his angels to speak to you. In your own Bible, he speaks to the leaders and warns them, and guides them through many perils.

When nations are in conflict with each other, God speaks in many ways. The supreme expression on

Earth of the word of God was the voice of his Son, the *Master Jesus*. Jesus spoke with the authority of God's words. Every word the Master spoke, every action the Master took, was for the good of the world. He was for all nations and creeds, as well as for the individual soul. So this tells you how God sees nations.

Joseph: Thank you, Titus.

Chou Speaks His Truth

Two days later…

Joseph: Hi, Chou! Thank you for coming to speak with me.

Chou: Greetings, Joseph! How are you?

Joseph: I'm very well, thank you, Chou. Titus tells me how busy you are these days.

Chou: Yes, and I am in a teaching role right now – a bit like you are. I have been giving lessons in how to help souls when they come to this side of life – how to deal in a loving and special way with all the different situations a soul may find itself in.

Joseph: Well, I don't envy you. I have problems teaching basic subjects to humans.

Chou: Yes, but my job is easier, because I've been in it for many, many years.

Joseph: Well, I hope you earn a good crust up

there!

Titus was telling me how God sees us, and I felt very humble when I realised how God speaks to us in a personal way. To God I must seem very dense, because you, as his enlightened souls, come and tell me the right ways to live my life, yet I go on my merry way, making the most stupid blunders.

Chou: Don't be so hard on yourself, Joseph. If *we* can put up with you, I'm sure *you* can.

Joseph: Um… I'm not sure how you mean that, Chou.

Chou: Many a true word is spoken in jest.

Joseph: Chou, before we start on this chat, may I tell people something about you?

Chou: I noticed you were writing about me for one of your other books. Let's not bore everyone with more. Hee-hee-hee!

Joseph: Yes, but I basically just talked about our first meeting, and little else besides.

Chou: Well, if you feel that you must.

Joseph: Thank you.

I hope you won't mind, dear Reader, if I digress awhile. Chou is, to my mind, the most wonderful teacher and friend that any human being could wish for. Through all his dealings with me and with others, we have truly come to love him. His sense of humour and fun are a source of inspiration. And I've never known him to be any other way. Over the years there have been many occasions when he would have been within his rights to despair of me and of others, but he has held steadfast and helped. Chou's position is that of a guide, but he trains others to become guides, too. Over the years I have spoken with many of the guides he has trained, and they all say he was and is a great soul to work with. I couldn't agree with them more. Thank you, Reader, for your patience.

Chou: Well, thank you, Joseph! I'll try to squeeze my head through the door, shall I? Hee-hee-hee!

Joseph: Chou, do the guides all get on together? Do they ever have disagreements with each other?

Chou: We don't have disagreements, but we have debates. Even on international spiritual matters, we are all working to the same ends. Of course we have our own ways of doing things, and as individuals we put plans into action according to the experience we have gained. As you are fond of saying, Joseph, "If I don't know the answer, I know someone who does." So we are covered for every eventuality.

Joseph: As a guide, giving service to the world, what are your ultimate aims?

Chou: To attain my spiritual development by serving your world and mine. In doing so, to bring the two worlds together in understanding and love, and to unite your world so that you understand each other better.

Joseph: Wow! When you throw a punch you take no prisoners, do you, Chou! But it seems to me that on a personal level you have already attained much of what you wish for.

Chou: We can always do better. And we must always strive to help others. By helping others, through the love of God, we also help ourselves.

Joseph: You know, in my world, we are told it is wrong for us to speak to the dead – that only evil can come of it. And you know from your experience in dealing with me, and with others too over the years, how agonising it has been for us. You have seen how we have torn into our emotional selves, because we have wanted to reach heaven and be children of God, and not distance ourselves from him.

Chou: I understand you ask this question for the book, and I am happy to answer. Throughout the ages humans have needed a deity or deities who they feel can respond to their inner selves and take away any guilt they have. And they have needed a

God or gods who can see and feel what they cannot express for themselves. Alongside this, people have always felt the need to speak to their loved ones beyond the moment of physical death. In primitive peoples, giving expression to this need took all kinds of forms. But as the human race advanced, its ideas changed. Societies developed, and they enriched themselves and their cultures with various ideas of a God. They were gradually moving forward towards understanding God, but in doing so, in many ways they removed God from their lives. Over time, and with different influences and many fears, God became an untouchable to humans. Much was based on the personal guilt of the leaders. It then began to be said that it was wrong to speak to any soul other than God.

You know, of course, that the Master Jesus spoke much about the life to come. His life was and is spent teaching the human race how to live our lives so we can attain the spiritual home God meant for us. Remember, Jesus said you must discern the spirit and put it to the test. Each and every one of you is a spiritual person capable of thinking deep thoughts. You must each decide for yourself what actions to take in your life. You should also remember this:

It is said that religions bring down nations, but faith saves souls.

Joseph: Thank you, Chou. Spirit have always spoken so well of God and his great love for us, as you well know. And Spirit have always given me – and many others over the years – truths that we have been able to verify in many different ways.

I have been asked many times in my life what happens to you when you pass from this world. Please, for the sake of those who wish to know, would you explain?

Chou: I could, but I will let someone speak who deals with this reality every day. You should write more books, Joseph, because you've been listening for a change!

Sarah Speaks Her Truth

Joseph: Hello, Sarah. Welcome! Chou said someone would come to help me explain a very important subject – what happens to our souls after we leave the mortal coil. Thank you very much! And I'd also be very interested to hear something about you.

Sarah: Hello, Joseph. It's a pleasure to speak to you, and I'll try to help as much as I can.

I have always worked with people, and with – as you call us – Spirit. And I have always been interested in ways of healing the mind and the body. So I studied psychology. Then I went on to study how the system of receiving souls works.

Joseph: May I interrupt you, Sarah? What did you need to do to convince your teachers you were suited to this kind of work? In my world, having studied does not necessarily mean you're the best person for a particular job.

Sarah: Even before I studied psychology, I had done work connected with soul arrivals for many years. So when the time came, I really was sure what I wanted to do.

Joseph: Thank you, Sarah. So what does happen to our souls when we arrive in the world of Spirit?

Sarah: When a soul is about to leave the mortal coil, loved ones gather and special helpers appear to assist the transition.

Joseph: Excuse me, Sarah. Does this happen for all people, irrespective of their faith or belief, and for non-believers too? And does the same thing happen for good *and* bad souls?

Sarah: Yes, it does, because the love of God is un-conditional, as has been explained to you.

Before the cord of life breaks, most people become aware that there are spirit people around them. On the other hand, there are some people who are not aware of anyone during this time. But as soon as the soul departs, it sees the loved ones and helpers who have gathered on the other side of life. Then the soul travels through a cleansing light.

Joseph: Is this the same light that is described by people who have had a near-death experience?

Sarah: Yes.

Joseph: I'm sorry to keep interrupting you, Sarah, but you said that all souls travel with help, and through a light. But some souls I have spoken to say they didn't see a light on their journey to the after-life. How do you account for this?

Sarah: Every soul passes through the light, but some have no recollection of it. There are many different factors at play; for example, the ability of a soul to be fully aware of its state. It may for one reason or another have closed its mind to what has happened to it. If you ask these souls how they got here, they will say, "I don't know", or "I can't remember". But they only *seem* not to recall any light, because of their closed minds.

Joseph: Thank you, Sarah.

Sarah: Then the soul goes to the place that is most suitable for it. For instance, enlightened souls go where it is easiest for them to accept their state. This is generally where there are friends and family whom the soul immediately recognises and accepts. The soul knows it has passed to the higher world, because here is its… whoever it may be. Other souls need more time to adjust before they can accept their new state, so they go to places where they are offered the kind of help they need to come to terms with their transition.

Joseph: Are there souls who never accept their state?

Sarah: For some it takes a long, long time. But time has no importance in our world, so we can be patient until they are ready to move on.

Joseph: Do all souls eventually come to realise and accept that they have passed into your world?

Sarah: No. If this were so, our work would be very easy. Some choose to go off and do what they feel is for them. In our world, far more than in yours, there is freedom of choice. But we persist, and try to help them. The edict that *we* follow is the *law of God*, and that is to *never give up on a soul, for every soul is a child of God.*

Joseph: Are we judged on how we have lived our lives?

Sarah: Up to a point, but the best judges are the souls themselves, because in our world realising one's sins is a far more powerful process than it is in yours. Because of the love and truth that abound, souls soon become aware that they cannot hide their sins from their fellow souls.

Joseph: Wow! I find that scary, Sarah.

Sarah: As do many, I assure you.

Joseph: What about really dark souls? Do they respond to this system?

Sarah: Some do, some do not. Those that don't soon find themselves in very strange circumstances.

Joseph: Could you go into more detail, please?

Sarah: Well, they try to hide from truth, but in doing so they go into what we call the shadows, and meet like souls who are eager for company. These souls spin many untruths to hold on to their new companions. As you can perhaps imagine, a kind of comfort can come about when you take shelter from truth together. You accept any port in a storm, as the saying goes.

Joseph: So if you stand up and profess your sins, however great they are, what happens to you?

Sarah: You are helped to atone for them. I assure you, there are no easy options. To the soul concerned, the sins may seem to take forever to atone for.

Joseph: What if someone committed murders, or perhaps ordered murders to take place, say a person like Hitler? The system you speak of sounds like it is geared to helping sinners. What about the victims and the loved ones who are left behind to deal with it all?

Sarah: I realise you ask these questions for the book you are writing. Do not believe that we help one more than the other. For the benefit of other people, I will explain how the system works:

Victims are helped in such a way as to relieve their suffering. Their pain is not like the pain they would feel in your world. We send in the most powerful souls to assist them, so they adjust far more quickly. The love they are given soon helps to bring them peace and comfort. The ones left behind also receive our love and care. We try to help by feeding them thoughts of their loved ones and conveying that they are at peace. We often direct these thoughts of love and comfort into their dreams, and we also put positive thoughts into their minds. This way we can calm the soul. Also, when we are able to, we channel healing to them, to help them further. We never interfere with the grieving process because that helps to heal.

Joseph: Are sinners made to face their victims?

Sarah: That mainly depends on the victim and their reasoning for wanting to confront the sinner, because we would not want victims to become sinners by default, through no fault of their own.

Joseph: Thank you, Sarah, for all your good advice and help. If it's OK, I would like to take these questions further at a later date. I'm afraid the body and mind are growing weary now.

Sarah: Thank you, too, Joseph. As the old saying goes, the spirit is willing but the flesh is weak.

Joseph: That is very true in my case – the decrepit body *is* weak.

Sarah: I bite my tongue, I am a lady, but Chou says he agrees with you.

Joseph: Yes, he would. Thank you, my friend. Good night and God bless, and love to you all.

A Blue Brother Speaks His Truth

Blue brothers and blue sisters are souls who have amassed truly vast amounts of knowledge. They have had many, many eons of experience working as senior guides, that is to say, guides who train other guides. They travel to every level of the divine world, and give advice on every aspect of life. They are highly trained in their own specialist fields. Blue brothers and blue sisters are also what you would describe as top spiritual barristers, who are incapable of bending the rules to suit the client or themselves. These wonderful souls are now the keepers of the laws of God's creation.

How wonderful to have an incorruptible legal system! Earth's legal systems, please take note.

Joseph: Hello! I'm very pleased to meet you. Thank you for coming to speak with me. I'm well aware how busy you are, so I'll try not to keep you too long; Chou tells me I tend to waffle a lot…

Blue Brother: It's my pleasure to be here! I always enjoy talking with people from your world.

Joseph: I've got so many questions I want to ask, it's hard to know where to start.

Blue Brother: Yes, I've been warned you like to know every possible detail. Were you one of those children who took clocks apart to see how they worked and then couldn't put them back together again?

Joseph: I can see who's been talking to you! Chou, no doubt! Anyway, for my first question, can you tell me if seraphs, angels, archangels and highly evolved souls readily make contact with human beings? Or does there need to be a momentous occasion for this to occur?

Blue Brother: They do not make contact with humans particularly often, although on occasion an angel will appear to a person, for varying reasons.

Joseph: Could you please give an example?

Blue Brother: Sometimes when a soul calls out in prayer, or from deep inside its being, a system kicks in that reminds me a bit of your e-mail servers. The person calling out opens up the right channels, and the message gets through to the right person to do the job. I could fill volumes describing the many different reasons why we make contact.

Joseph: I would like to ask you about destiny. On Earth, we tend to believe that we have a predetermined future, and that we set the stage for the life we wish to live before we come into the world. There are religions that say we do this many times over. This means reincarnation. But the church I grew up with tells us this is wicked and evil, and that we would be putting our souls in danger by holding such beliefs.

Blue Brother: I am well aware that you do not subscribe to the church's point of view in any way. Destiny is certainly a truth. Because we are all children of God, and each one of us is a part of his great plan, many things are predestined for each soul. A loving father does not send his children into the world unprepared. With a great deal of preparation and much guidance, the soul is able to discern what the best way will be for it to fulfil its destiny. For example, some souls choose to be artists, as they feel this is the best way to serve God and themselves.

Of course there is reincarnation. Do you think that a power of the immensity of God would limit a part of his creation to one twinkling-of-an-eye existence we call life, and then just let it lie dormant until atonement day? No. What would be the point? God is an active and ever-creative deity. All things he creates are given the chance to go from strength to strength. So it is very little trouble to allow a soul to keep returning, to serve through action. All thinking faiths are aware that reincarnation is a part of the human need to succeed, and that through the grace of God, people are given many opportunities to fulfil their destinies.

Joseph: Yes. But you try talking to the established churches about reincarnation. You would be met with a stake and a hammer at the ready, to do holy justice to the wickedness you believe in.

Blue Brother: Belief is not built in a day. And remember, the Son of God was crucified for his beliefs. If you read your Bible you will find many stories of reincarnation.

Joseph: The churches would have us believe that only enlightened souls can return, to serve mankind.

Blue Brother: I would refer you to my earlier answers.

Joseph: Should the churches be challenged about this matter?

Blue Brother: Why should they be? Time challenges Man, and ideas change. You only need to look at human history to know this is true.

Joseph: It seems to me that if you bang the drum long and loud enough you get heard, and your faith is accepted.

Blue Brother: An empty bottle makes quite a sound when the wind passes over it, but does it convey anything other than an empty noise?

Joseph: Um… point taken.

Could I ask you, please, what are the most important aspects of life that we should be concerned with to help us evolve into spiritual beings?

Blue Brother: At the beginning of this conversation you said you would try not to keep me too long. To answer your questions to my satisfaction, I would be here for weeks, or months or years, talking nonstop.

Joseph: Er… point taken, again.

Blue Brother: The best answer is this: Do not do as others would do. Do as Jesus would do. Be kind and loving, and bear charity in your hearts. Do not do to others what you would not expect to have done to yourself.

Joseph: Thank you for your time and patience.

Blue Brother: Where I can help my fellow souls, there I shall be. Peace and joy to your world, and

God's blessings on you all.

There is no doubt that some of the answers I get could fill many volumes. Sometime in the future, when I have caught up with myself, I will compile more books of knowledge from the divine world: questions, answers, and truths.

Titus and I Have
A Chat about Healing

Joseph: Hi, Titus! How are you?

Titus: I'm fine, and I'm looking forward to talking with you. So please try not to waffle. You know I like straight talking.

Joseph: That's great, that is. We haven't even started our chat yet, and already you're dictating how it should go.

Titus: See what I mean! Waffle, waffle…

Joseph: Er, um, yes. Can we talk about healing, please?

Titus: Yes, of course. It is a subject that is very dear to me, as you know.

Joseph: There are hundreds and hundreds of kinds of healing. Everywhere you look you can see it taking place. People being kind to each other is a form of healing. Music is a great healer, as I well know, Titus, because whenever I have a headache I can listen to music and feel better in no time at all. There is deep spiritual healing, faith healing, medical healing, and now there is crystal healing.

Titus: Make your point. I'm growing old here.

Joseph: Sorry. How does healing work?

Titus: The whole of the spiritual and physical world is based on the renewal of life. God's love of his creation is never-ending. Therefore his creation is always expanding. God's energies are such that life is forever regenerating. Anything that may malfunction, in the fullness of time, becomes whole again. That is why it is ridiculous to say that the spirit ceases to function once it has left the mortal coil. How could it expect to become whole again if it lay dormant until Judgement Day?

Joseph: Wow, Titus! You've opened a big can of worms with that last statement.

Titus: Truth is truth however it may rock the boat. Truth should make great waves.

Joseph: Can everything in this world and your world be put right by healing?

Titus: Yes, it can. People should remember that love, kindness and understanding are very great healers, too.

Joseph: Do you have to be a spiritual person, or a very good person, or know about the divine world in order to be a healer?

Titus: You don't need to be any of these things. God's love does not make merit of the regard a person is held in on Earth, but rather of the goodwill of one person towards another. Even people of the jungles, who do not know God as you know him, have the gift of healing. Remember, healing is the grace of God. It is from the endless renewing of God's creation that the energies for healing are drawn.

Joseph: So how does spiritual healing work?

Titus: Spiritual healing is carried out with the help of an outside agent, for example a healing guide. This means a spirit who specialises in this form of healing, helping the mortal person to concentrate the energies that are needed.

Joseph: What about faith healing? How does that work?

Titus: The basis of faith healing is a person's belief that either God or the universal energies will heal. Or, in the case of organised faiths, that collective prayer will bring about healing. Remember, Joseph, that thoughts are living things, so they have an energy, which can draw on the greater energy that God has provided.

Joseph: I believe that our Saviour is the greatest healer. Surely all we need to do is ask in his name, and we will receive the Creator's gifts, for the benefit of whoever is in need.

Titus: Of course the Master is the greatest of healers. But you must remember there are many faiths in your world, and all of them lead to God in their own way. God is a great respecter of all creeds that follow the principle of doing good for people, for the greater glory of all life. You can see this by looking at his creation. The human condition is so diverse. God allows free will where human development is concerned, so that each soul may move towards spiritual growth and fulfilling its needs. This does not detract from the Master's power in any way at all. Indeed, it underlines his wisdom, and his love of all humanity and all life. For the Master is the supreme energy which is God. He is the fulfilment of the promise of God that through faith, mountains can be moved. So, to return to your first question, healing, in its many different forms, is a gift which flows from God's renewal of his creation.

Joseph: Thank you, Titus, for the information. You have given me plenty to think about.

Woe is Me!

Joseph: Hello, is anyone listening to me? Hello!? All out today, are we? I see. When I want to talk, all I get is the cold shoulder!

Please note, Reader, I do sometimes have a day of being a juvenile. "I'm so hard done by…" "I need to be listened to…" "Woe is me…"

Spirit: Yes, we're here. We'll sit and listen, if we must.

Joseph: Well, thank you for coming, I'm much obliged. Who am I speaking to?

Spirit: There's a group of us here. We've learned from past experience that when you're in this frame of mind it's better to come in a group, otherwise you tend to rave on and on and on.

Joseph: OK, I get the message, thank you very much. But who am I speaking to now?

Spirit: I am James.

Joseph: Do I know you?

James: No, I volunteered to speak with you. So did the others who are here with me.

Joseph: Well, what I want to say is this: I really feel I'm going nowhere fast. I do a lot of learning and a lot of meeting people. But this only seems to lead to me passing on information, telling people about the spirit world, and telling them about their relatives and friends on the divine side of life. Of course I know this is important in its own way, but I don't feel I am serving as I should.

James: We all serve according to our understanding of God's will. In the fullness of time, we are directed by God to carry out his wishes. We tend to call this our destiny.

Joseph: So you are saying that we are all born to a destiny?

James: Yes, of course. Many fail to fulfil it, but God in his mercy allows us many chances, so that ultimately we can succeed in our spiritual growth. So be happy, Joseph, that you're where you're at, and consider yourself very privileged to be serving in the way you are.

Joseph: OK, James, I will. It has definitely cheered

me up to hear that. Thank you.

May I please ask you a question about how we choose the families we are born to, if we do at all?

James: If I tried to answer that question in the detail it deserves, you'd be writing another ten books, and even then you wouldn't have explained it all.

Joseph: Well, could you give me the bare bones, then?

James: I will let a friend of mine who is here with the group explain it to you, as this is her subject.

Joseph: Thank you for your help, James. You have made me feel so much better. Sorry I was such a wet blanket.

Mona: Hello, I am Mona. And this is my friend Andrew, who is also an expert on this subject. Andrew would like to speak to you, too.

Joseph: Thank you both for coming to talk to me. I have always been fascinated to know why we are born to one family and not another. Of course Spirit have explained the subject to me to some degree over the years, but with so many other things going on in my life, I have never had the time until now to put pen to paper.

Mona and Andrew: As you well know, the driving force in most people's lives, both in the divine world and the physical world, is continuous spiritual development. Therefore, while you are still in the "school of life" of the divine world, you formulate a plan to help you achieve your aims when you are back in the physical world. Once you have somewhat plotted this course, you then look around to see what environment would best propel you towards reaching your goals. In other words, what family and circumstances to be born into.

Joseph: Do you get any help in deciding?

Mona and Andrew: Yes, to a degree, but remember there is also free will involved. We can give advice, but we cannot say what choices to make.

Joseph: I feel I can't have listened to any advice when I chose the family I was born into, because none of them were remotely interested in the divine world, although now that they're getting on a bit, they're starting to get the notion that there is something beyond their bank balances. But I think it would have been a good idea to choose a normal, spiritual, family environment to help me reach the goals I had set for myself, instead of going round the houses like I have. Still, like Titus and Chou always say, I suppose I do waffle a lot before I get to whatever I'm trying to say or do.

Mona and Andrew: Looking back on your life, were there not some members of your family who helped you reach certain goals?

Joseph: I'm sorry, I may seem ungrateful, but what kind of help are you talking about? I'm not consciously aware that there was any.

Mona and Andrew: When you were in your teens, one of your sisters stood up for you against the family when they were deriding your work with us. And through their ways, your family helped to show you how not to live.

Joseph: But surely with their influence, I could have followed them and become like them. After all, I was the youngest, and perhaps the most impressionable.

Mona and Andrew: Ha! Don't make us laugh. You have always been the most stubborn person. Always have been and always will be, you.

Joseph: Excuse me, but I consider myself quite an approachable person, willing to change my opinions when I need to.

Mona and Andrew: Oh, really?! Well, shall we get on with answering your questions..?

It may not always seem that people have made the right choices with their families. But you must remember that a family is chosen both for the potential it holds for the life of the child that is to be born into it, and for the spiritual development of everyone involved in the greater family circle.

Joseph: Huh! My family?! Spiritual?

Mona and Andrew: Your grandmother has just arrived to sit in on this discussion.

Joseph: Hello, Nanna! I'm so thrilled you're here!

Mona and Andrew: Your grandmother sends her love. She asks if you recall the conversations you had together when she was on Earth. She used to tell you that you must never stop listening to Spirit, because Spirit want you to develop yourself.

Joseph: Yes! I always felt Nanna knew things that were far beyond this world, because she always talked so much about the Master and how much she was looking forward to going to meet him. Nanna fully believed what the Bible said, and all the promises Jesus made to us. And Nanna was the one person on Earth who encouraged me to go on and trust in my spirit friends. Of course Nanna's belief and Spirit's teachings coincided, because Spirit have always held the teachings of the Master in supreme regard. So from my point of view, Nanna was the reason why I chose the family I did. Well, one of the main reasons.

Could you please answer another question for me?

Mona and Andrew: We would be happy to.

Joseph: Right from when I was very young, Spirit have taught me always to work hard, and to love and care for everyone, regardless of their state or their creed. But in truth, there are some members of my family that I don't love, and sometimes I feel very guilty about it. Is this a great weakness in me?

Mona and Andrew: Has it stopped you from helping them when help was needed?

Joseph: Well, no, but I would help anyone who asked me. Everyone has that quality to some degree or other. But I don't think it has very much to do with love.

Mona and Andrew: Yes, it does. It has everything to do with love – love of the highest order – because you are asking nothing in return.

Joseph: So are you saying that love does not necessarily have to be a feeling? Love could be an action you take in a situation you happen to find yourself in?

Mona and Andrew: To some degree, yes. A family is a group of souls who have come together for one reason or another. Each member is an individual, and each individual is different. So how could you be expected to feel exactly the same love for each one? No; you must reach out to your higher self and love each one in the spiritual sense, as you have learned from your faith and from the teachings of God's love. Do this in life, and you will have learned a great lesson.

Joseph: I do pray for people who have done evil things in the world, but when I pray for, say, mass murderers or child killers, I don't have the same feeling, or the depth of feeling that I have when I pray for someone I love. Does God still accept my prayers, knowing that there are times when I am praying out of duty to my beliefs?

Mona and Andrew: Yes, of course he does. God is fully aware of your imperfections. That's why you always say your prayers through Jesus Christ the Lord. You know full well that you need a spiritual booster to carry your prayers for you, and that Christ will put in for you what you cannot put in for yourself. Keep working on your spirituality, Joseph. Don't expect to become one of the giants of total enlightenment. One day, maybe, if we go by the adage that hope springs eternal! Hee hee! We're only jesting with you now. But what we can say to you is this: Strive to become the best you can, but always keep your feet on the ground. Always do things in life that give help, hope and love of the highest order, and serve without reward.

Joseph: Thank you both so much for your God-inspired advice. Please tell Nanna I love her very much and she's still my heroine.

Don't worry, Reader, I haven't gone all religious on you, but I have to say that right now I feel more uplifted than I have for a while. See what a good moan can do for you!

Life Forms As Yet Unknown

Joseph: Hello? Please may I speak to someone who knows about all the different life forms, both seen and unseen, that live in the universe?

Morgan: Hello! My name is Morgan.

Joseph: Hello, Morgan. It's very nice to see you, and to speak with you. Thank you for coming to answer my questions. I'll try to make them sound as sensible as I can. It's funny – people tell me I'm quite bright, but when I speak with Spirit I always feel like I'm some kind of underdeveloped amoeba. Oh, well…

I understand that there are different levels of awareness in the spirit world. But is there more to the spirit world than this?

Morgan: Yes. Apart from the levels which your world calls the lower planes, there are also in-between planes that exist for those souls who are not yet ready to make a jump forward. Just as in your world, where some of you are afraid of what you don't know and wait to see what develops before you make a move, so these in-between planes act as waiting rooms for the unsure. These souls eventually feel ready make a move, and then go on their merry way. I am giving you a simplified answer, of course, otherwise I will be here until you are too old to hold a pen.

Joseph: Are there such things as extraterrestrial beings? Of course I know there are, as I have met up with some – against my own personal wishes, I might add. Still, that's another story.

Morgan: Why ask, then, if you already know?

Joseph: As I have explained to other friends from the divine world who have come to speak with me, often in the past I have simply not been in the right situation or had the time to make a written record of the things that Spirit tell me. Besides, many people have a great interest in this kind of subject, myself included.

Morgan: Yes, there are many thousands of different life forms in your universe alone, and certainly in the divine world too. God's creation did not just stop at the earth world – it goes on into infinity. Your world is a part of that creation, but not the whole of it. Many life forms have developed in a way that is beyond the understanding of your peoples, so naturally their physical appearance can be vastly different from yours. People in your world who have seen beings who are not of earth sometimes say they look like monsters, or unlike anything they can relate to. But I can assure you, earth people look just as strange to them.

Joseph: Could you please tell me about other forms of life in your world?

Morgan: Well, they have also evolved according to their needs and through their own awareness to the form that suits them the best. The higher their spiritual awareness, the higher the form is in which they appear. That is to say, an evolved soul may appear as an angel, for example.

Joseph: Can extraterrestrials develop themselves spiritually to the point that they reach the status of an angel?

Morgan: Of course! Why should there only be forms of life that humans can understand? As I have said, *God's creation is so vast that all life evolves through his grace, and he gives all life time to perfect itself.* As others have already said to you, *God's love is* *so great that all life is equal in his sight.*

Joseph: Thank you, Morgan. Can I go on to ask you whether the different worlds mix, on your side of life?

Morgan: They can, of course, but in general they tend to stay in the environment they know and understand. It would be like me taking you to a world that was completely alien to you. You wouldn't even understand the basics that everyone around you was taking for granted, so you wouldn't know how to develop.

Joseph: St. John the Divine tells us of the great holocaust to come, and the appearance of strange forms of life.

Morgan: I'll stop you there. You would need to speak to someone much better qualified than me for the answer to that question, because now you are talking about something that is of immense importance to the universe. If I tried to tell you in a few lines, it would not be possible for me to explain the complexities of so great a matter. I might appear to give so little information that I could confuse people and cause much unhappiness. The great ones need to explain this to you, because so many good things go hand in hand with the real meaning of the knowledge which God imparted to St. John the Divine.

Joseph: Morgan, this is Impatient Joseph speaking. When can I ask for this information to be given?

Morgan: Well, I would suggest that it be sometime when you are wide awake and listening, for the details are long and many.

Joseph: I understand.

Morgan: I must take my leave now, but it has been a pleasure talking with you.

Joseph: Thank you, Morgan. I really have enjoyed our time together. I appreciate that we have only been able to touch on a few subjects, but do you think maybe in the future, we might be able to go into much more detail?

Morgan: I will be very happy to talk to you in greater detail on the subjects we have discussed, and plenty of others too.

Creation and Evolution

You will be well aware by now that I follow the theory of creation, and do not believe in the theory of evolution in its traditional sense, but I wanted to find out how the spirit world view the argument.

Joseph: Hello, Chou. Would it be possible to speak to someone who is knowledgeable about creation and evolution, please?

Chou: Yes, I was aware you were going to make that request, so I brought along a friend to speak with you. His name is Perkins.

Joseph: Thank you, Chou.

Hello, Perkins. That's an unusual name you have!

Perkins: Hello, Joseph! It's a pleasure to meet you at last. I have been told much about you. Yes, my name has been passed down the generations of my family.

Now, as to whether we are the product of creation or evolution, the answer is as follows: We are the product of both, in the fullest sense. Creation means that an intelligence brings something into existence, with a definite aim in mind, whereas evolution means that things develop at random, and the result is whatever happens to transpire.

Joseph: Excuse me, Perkins, but you will soon learn about me. I sometimes need a bit of help to join up the dots... I still don't see how the two are connected.

Perkins: You have jumped ahead of me. I will explain it to you, if you give me time!

Joseph: Sorry, Perkins. I consider myself rebuked.

Perkins: Not to worry. Anyway, as I was saying, creation is the way that God formed all things, with a definite purpose in mind. But within that creation, God also allowed the development of certain things to take place in a way that would allow freedom of expression and a measure of independence. God was well aware that the physical world needed to develop in this way, so that when life appeared on Earth, he could allow the imperfections to evolve into perfection. He is not a God who makes puppets on a string.

Already he was showing us his immaculate love, even if to our minds he was somewhat compromising his majesty for the sake of the souls who were yet to be born. So yes, to some extent, the earth was allowed to evolve. The evolution of the dinosaurs was a part of that process, and so were many other events and periods of time that have been important to life, all over the universe. But always remember that everything has a purpose. In the beginning there was a plan, and therefore it is clear that there is a creative process. And please bear in mind that what I am giving you now is a very simplified synopsis.

Joseph: Thank you very much, Perkins, and yes, I will.

May I ask you a question about beings from other planets?

Perkins: Go ahead.

Joseph: We are told that we are made in the image of God, but what about extraterrestrials? Are they made in the image of God too? If they are, why do some of them look so unimaginably different from us? Is it just that they have evolved to their present form, as we have done?

Perkins: God has no shape or form. When it is said that God created man in his own image, this is not a reference to physical forms in any way. Being made in God's image has a far deeper meaning than your world tends to think, and that meaning is spiritual. *All* life is in the form that God wants it to be in. The Earth needs to start thinking beyond its own little world and expanding its mind to a greater awareness of all things, seen and unseen.

Joseph: Thank you so much, Perkins. It has been a great joy to talk with you.

Diseases. Why?

Joseph: Hello, Piarna!

Piarna and I go back a long way – right to my early days with Spirit. Piarna has been a source of help and comfort to me through the years.

Piarna: Hello, Joseph. How are you? I hear on the grapevine that you're taking up writing.

Joseph: Yes, that's right. People keep telling me I should write about my experiences with the spirit world. And Spirit keep saying how interesting it would be for people. So… we'll see! Anyway, Piarna, I would like to talk to you about why we have diseases in the world, if I may.

Piarna: Yes, of course.

Joseph: Thank you.

Piarna: Germs and viruses all have their part to play in the creative and evolutionary development of the universe.

Joseph: Excuse me for interrupting you, Piarna, but when you think about God's vast knowledge and creative abilities, surely there should be no need for these forms of life to exist.

Piarna: God's plan is such that all things in his creation are relevant to all life. What humans must remember is that not all life revolves around them. Things are not bad simply because they don't fit in with the well-being of the human race. All life has a purpose.

Joseph: But a lot of these things mutate and cause dreadful havoc in the world.

Piarna: What you need to understand is that all life needs to fulfil its potential. What may be destructive to one form of life is an ally to another, so in the fullness of time, all forms of life will be compatible.

Joseph: So all these things are in the creative-evolutionary plan?

Piarna: Absolutely. At this stage of the creative-evolutionary plan, all is not yet revealed. However in the fullness of time God's plans will become clear. What your world needs to understand, Joseph, is this: God's creation of life is for the total benefit of all life forms. It is not for the benefit of himself. God is knowledge, and purity of mind and soul. His love is so great that we can only guess at the breadth of his understanding and compassion, so there cannot be any kind of malice in him. Also you must remember it is *souls* that are saved, not physical forms; in your world you are told by wise teachers not to lay up for yourselves treasures on earth, where moth and rust corrupt.

Joseph: I hear what you are saying, but to people on earth, the loss of a loved one in these circumstances is very distressing indeed – people have been known to lose faith in God, some of whom are definitely very nice people.

Piarna: Of course this is true, and as you well know, Joseph, we do everything in our power to help people who suffer in any way through tragic circumstances. But do not confuse emotions with the path of creation. The two are intermingled through the processes of God's love for all his creation. But whereas emotions are based on personal feelings and love from an individual, creation relates to the sum total of all life, for all time. Life is never based solely on the existences people lead on earth. Life is, rather, an intertwining of mortal life with life beyond the veil; if this were not so I would not be able to speak to you now. So yes, to lose a loved one in any circumstances is extremely distressing for human beings, but the truth is that the departed have taken their promotion to a higher state of life, and the day comes when great loves meet again. You know this to be true, Joseph.

Joseph: Indeed I do, Piarna. But that leads me to another question I am often asked. What happens if you have had more than one partner on earth, for example if a person has been married two or three times? Which one do you meet up with? Or what if a relationship you had was a very unhappy one? Do you meet the person again who you were so unhappy with?

Piarna: That's simple to answer. "Till death do us part" means that once a soul has passed into our world, it really does have free will. Therefore you only meet those that you want to meet, whether that means one partner or several. The choice is yours.

Joseph: I see. But what if one partner wants to meet and the other doesn't? Where's the choice in that?

Piarna: There is a choice, because each person is free to decide whether or not to meet up with their earthly partner. If a person wishes there to be no meeting, then there is no meeting, and the partner will have to respect this. But there are always people on hand to help resolve difficult situations, if help is needed.

Joseph: Thank you so much, Piarna. It has been wonderful to talk with you again. Please come back and see me as soon as you can. I love spending time with you. And you explain everything in such an easy way. Hopefully one day I'll feel as comfortable as you do dealing with such a breadth of knowledge.

Piarna: What a flatterer! Are you going soft in the head? But thank you, Joseph, and I will come back as soon as my job allows me to.

Piarna teaches in the university of spiritual awareness. She is also, I am told, a very good artist.

Trance

For many years now I have been able to go into a state of trance with the assistance of Spirit. This entails me sitting in a cosy chair in a room that is warm and welcoming and illuminated with soft lights. Please note from the outset that I have never sat in a darkened room asking, "Is there anybody there?" Séances definitely never have been and never will by my style. If I ever stumbled across that sort of thing I would be out of the room like a shot. I would never be involved in that kind of set-up.

When I am in trance, I am in an unconscious state and therefore unaware of my surroundings. Because of this, I can only pass on to you what other people who are present at sittings recount to me. And I can assure you I am the most sceptical of people, and often find it difficult to accept what they tell me.

Every meeting starts with prayers. This includes the Lord's Prayer. We go on to thank God for his many mercies upon us all, then we pray for the human race, asking for God's blessings on people in each and every circumstance in which human lives are lived. And of course we pray for the animal kingdom and for Mother Earth.

I have asked one of the sitters to describe what happens as I am going into trance, before any spirit has come to speak.

Sitter: There are a few minutes' silence, and then trance begins. We know that a change is taking place when your facial expressions alter. You always go very cold, too, which is why we make sure you have a blanket, or the heating is turned up higher than usual. Then you sit up very straight, you fold your arms as if into wide sleeves, and a big, beaming smile appears on your face.

That smile is Chou-Li's. Chou-Li always comes first, to tell us that you are fine and everything is ready to start. He always begins by saying "Greetings!" in a very Chinese-sounding way, and then he says, "God bless you all." Next he speaks to each of us in turn, asking us how we all are. The wonderful thing about Chou is the warm, happy feeling he gives to us all.

He is always very cheerful, and never any different.

Chou then goes on to say there are many people waiting to talk with us, and in his own inimitable way he reassures us that he is in charge and all is well.

Joseph: How do you know all this is not just me putting on an act?

Sitter: Your face changes, in a physical way.

Joseph: What do you mean?

Sitter: Well, somehow the bone structure appears to change, and the face takes on a different shape from yours.

Not only that, but sometimes you are put into positions that in your conscious state you would be physically unable to achieve.

Joseph: Huh? Could you explain, please?

Sitter: Well, sometimes you are put into yogic postures. Other times your body is placed so that you are sitting the way an Indian sits to relax, and with the greatest respect, Joseph, your body is not that of an Adonis in all his glory – more like old clay gone hard.

Joseph: I needed reminding of that…

Sitter: Very often people speak to us in foreign languages, both ancient and modern. I've lost count of how many different languages I've heard.

Joseph: How do you know it's not me speaking these languages? After all, if they are ancient, no one would know them; I could just be making them up...

Sitter: Well, there are a few reasons. First of all, everyone that knows you knows what a struggle you often have even with English.

Joseph: I needed reminding of that, too!

Sitter: As far as ancient languages are concerned, sometimes the speaker will manage to utter the modern English name of his or her language. We may have read of the existence of the language in history books, or be able to find out something about it on the internet. Usually speakers also try to provide a couple of other basic facts in English about where and when they lived so that we can understand something about their backgrounds. If they can't, Chou often steps in and does a quick interpreting job. As regards modern languages, one of the sitters is a linguist, and has often identified the language being spoken, and has sometimes conversed with speakers in their own language.

Joseph: I wonder, of the hundreds of transcripts you have made over the years, if you might choose one at random so that the reader may have some idea of what a conversation between a spirit person and a human is like.

Sitter: Well, it often sounds very much like any conversation between two humans, although when higher spirits talk, the subject matter can be pretty different from what you might overhear on the bus. Anyway, here is a transcript that mentions the ancient Egyptian pyramids. The spirit who was talking to us was, in that particular incarnation, one of the builders of the Great Pyramid of Giza, although he has lived many other lives since then. In his most recent incarnation, at the end of the nineteenth and in the early decades of the twentieth century, he wrote works which still enjoy great fame in our society.

The transcript begins here.

Sitter: Thank you very much for coming to speak with us. We are deeply honoured.

I have read some of your books. To me they are the most precious jewels of wisdom I have encountered in my life. Many times I have wondered whether all your life you were as spiritually refined and perfect as one could assume by reading your books.

Spirit: Like all people, I had to struggle to refine my spirituality.

Sitter: In your incarnation in ancient Egypt, what

was your role in the building of the Great Pyramid of Giza?

Spirit: Mine was a supervisory role.

Sitter: Could I be rather rude and ask you some questions about your personal life?

Spirit: Certainly.

Sitter: Firstly, could you tell me what your sexuality was in that life?

Spirit: Part of my destiny was to experience human life in all its rich diversity.

Sitter: Did you have a family?

Spirit: I had a wife, and three daughters.

Sitter: Could you please share with me some of your impressions of life back then?

Spirit: Life had a great beauty in its material and artistic aspects. Moreover, the whole society was imbued with a deep spirituality. Yet man's treatment of his fellow man, then as now, left much to be desired. The pyramids were built by forced labour. The ancient Egyptians' treatment of slaves was most often cruel in the extreme.

Sitter: Would you like to be reborn into our present-day world?

Spirit: The decades to come will see the most interesting chapter in the history of Earth, ever. There is much beauty in your world, but it is also a world that is thick with lies. I would accept to be reborn into it if I felt that I could make a positive contribution to Earth's spiritual development.

Transcript ends.

Joseph: Thank you very much. It was fascinating to read your transcript, even though I realise this was only a small part of it. I took a peek at the rest of it and got some idea of how many different personalities come to speak with you.

Sitter: They are all informative in their own way. But the two things that impress us the most about them are the way they care so deeply about the welfare of the world, and how wonderfully they speak of God's creation.

Joseph: What happens once they have all finished speaking?

Sitter: Well, before they do, there is nearly always someone who comes to talk to us about some aspect of spirituality, and leaves us with much to think about. And then you come back. Often you look like a fox that has been dragged backwards through a hedge.

Joseph: I'm not sure if I should say thank you or not.

The Bible

Please let me introduce my friend, Father Brown. Father Brown was a church minister in the West Midlands. He was born in 1891, and was a very great authority on the Bible.

Joseph: Welcome, Father Brown.

Father Brown: Good evening, Joseph. How are you feeling? I understand you have been rather poorly.

Joseph: I am much better now, Father, and thank you for asking. May I put some questions to you about the Bible, please?

Father Brown: Certainly you may.

Joseph: The Bible is the scripture of the Christian faith, and amongst other things, it contains much about how people should live their lives. The Bible is a very great work, there is no doubt about it. It is hugely important in the Christian faith, and there are many things in it which I personally hold very dear to my heart. But I don't accept everything that is written in the Bible. If I did, we would not be having this conversation now. Indeed, my talking to people who have passed into spirit, such as you, Father Brown, could be interpreted as being in touch with dark forces.

Hmm… Everyone is entitled to their own beliefs, I suppose…

And in an earlier age, it is very possible I would have been branded as a wizard and burned at the stake. Anyway, the point is, Father, am I wrong not to follow the Bible?

Father Brown: You have already said there are things about the Bible that you hold very dear to your heart. But you must live your life according to the path you are on. This, you pray, is to enlighten your soul. The Bible is one of the roads you can follow to lead to God.

Joseph: Well, Father, according to the Christian religion, the path I am on will lead me to ruin. And yet talking with people from your world has only ever brought happiness and goodness to my life.

Father Brown: Have you not answered your own

question? The paths that God offers for us to reach him are many and varied. So you treat the Bible with the great respect this work deserves, and continue in your faith in God and his goodness to you. You must develop spiritually far beyond a strict reliance on the Bible. Love must be the basis of your deeds – for it is by your deeds that you are known.

Joseph: Is the Bible factually correct?

Father Brown: Many parts of it are, although over the centuries it has undergone many additions and deletions.

Joseph: Is our reading of the Bible the same now as it was in years gone by?

Father Brown: As is the case with any great work, people will always put their own interpretations on it.

Joseph: How should we interpret the Bible?

Father Brown: We must always have our own heartfelt interpretations. Scholars will debate this and that, but the truth never changes, no matter how much words may be altered to suit the time or the people concerned.

Joseph: How important is the Old Testament to the New Order – to the teachings of Christ? The Old Testament is all hell and damnation, sacrifice and the wrath of God, whereas the New Testament teaches love, kindness, hope, and a life to look forward to. Through Christ, we now see that God is loving, forgiving, and ever aware of each one of us as an individual, as one of his children.

Father Brown: You prove my point very nicely about people making different interpretations according to the times and situations they find themselves in.

You and I both know God for his love of all life – a love that asks no rewards for itself, only rewards for us. So, as the saying goes: "You pays your money and you takes your choice." I know my choice is the teaching of Christ.

Joseph: Could you please answer a question that is very important to me personally?

Father Brown: Certainly.

Joseph: I try to ask this question to as many people as I can, especially when I know they have great knowledge and spirituality. On your travels, if I can put it that way, do you ever see Christ?

Father Brown: Christ is so important to our lives here, that yes, I do see him, because he is ever fulfilling the promise he made to mankind, that a home is being prepared for you. His love radiates everywhere.

Joseph: Do you see any of the other great souls

who have given so much to mankind?

Father Brown: Yes, absolutely. They too work continually for all life.

Joseph: Which world would you rather be in – this one, or the one you are in?

Father Brown: What a strange question that is, coming from you, Joseph! I live in the world I am meant to live in, and I work for the other.

Joseph: I'm sorry, Father. Really I was just wondering if there was anything you miss about this world, maybe something that is different on your side of life?

Father Brown: There are things about each world that I miss when I am in the other. Where I am now, there is not the confusion you have in your world. Here we feel the greater purpose of our lives much more keenly. We see our paths much more clearly. On the other hand, why do you think so many wish to return to your world to fulfil their destinies?

Joseph: I could go on all night asking you questions, Father, but my old body is very tired... I must go to sleep.

Father Brown: My old body went to sleep years ago! Good night, Joseph, and God bless. I'll speak to you soon.

Thelma, Edward and Motular

Joseph: Thank you all for coming to talk to me this evening. I've got a mixed bag of questions here to ask you, if you don't mind.

Thelma: Fire away.

Joseph: First of all, may I ask you if you think the world is in a worse state now than it has ever been, and if so, why?

Thelma: That is a question that would be very difficult for someone living in your world to answer, because personal experiences colour people's thoughts and feelings very much. Looking from this vantage point, I feel that people in the world are achieving something of a greater understanding of each other, but there is still a long way to go. Some progress has been made towards co-operation between different faiths. Many of your governments are held more accountable to the people than they once were.

Joseph: When I look around the world, though, I see much trouble, and people in great distress, for example through war.

Thelma: I did not say the world was perfect, I said many governments are held more accountable to the people than they were in the past. Often when a tyranny causes great suffering, others try to avert this, or step in to stop it.

To get back to your question, certainly the world has more ways of waging war than ever before, and more ways of killing people in vast numbers, but you have learned something from the two world wars of the twentieth century.

For me, the worst time in Earth's history was the Dark Ages, for people then were morally and spiritually dead. Those we needed to look up to were totally corrupt. It was only people's faith that saw them through.

Joseph: Thank you, Thelma. I share your optimism for the world.

My next question is this: We are supposed to be moving towards an age of enlightenment, when everything will come together spiritually. What does the divine world feel about this?

Edward: I would say that the age of enlightenment arrived when the Great Master walked your earthly world. *He* made the world more enlightened, as did the other great souls who came and gave your world its spiritual backbone again. The fact that societies become more modern does not mean that they become more advanced spiritually – indeed they often revert to those old chestnuts we call *greed* and *envy*. Usually it is the leaders who take the most – the poor have nothing to give. That is why it is said that it is easier for a camel to go through the eye of a needle, than for a rich man to enter into the kingdom of God.

In many ways, though, your world *is* in an age of enlightenment; I am thinking of the many advances in medical care, and the improvements to your social systems. These, in their different ways, are also a form of spiritual advancement.

Joseph: According to many of the prophets, and even the great seer Nostradamus, it is in this century that great disasters are to occur. We are often told that some event will cause a catastrophe – for example the turn of the millennium – but in most respects life carries on as normal.

Edward: Prophets and seers have always read the

signs; each one gives his or her own interpretation of events. Do not look to the signs of nature, but to the mysteries of God, for he will determine when they shall be.

Joseph: How does God see his children of today? I know I have asked this question before, but it is always interesting to hear different people's perspectives.

Edward: God always gives each of his children their due. The harder you work, the greater your reward is – the higher you ascend the spiritual ladder. God's love – and this has been said many times – is unconditional, so he sees each of his children according to their merits.

Joseph: May I ask you about people who commit suicide? We are told this is a wicked thing to do, but are individual circumstances taken into account?

Edward: I'll let Motular talk to you about that. I've found our meeting most enjoyable. We'll speak again soon.

Joseph: Thank you so much for talking to me.

Motular: Good evening, Joseph.

Joseph: Welcome, Motular. Can I ask, have I spelt your name right?

Motular: Yes, you have spelt it right.

Joseph: Do you mind me asking where you lived when you were on earth?

Motular: I lived in India, although it was a long time ago.

As far as suicide is concerned, God, through his great love, tells us *he* is the judge of all matters. He has given laws which men must live by. But he is also the one who decides when and how a person is judged, and this he does through his vast intellectual power, so that each is given to according to his or her need. Each soul is treated as an individual.

Joseph: It does seem to me that a lot of God's laws for the world have been made use of selectively by leaders to promote the views that they happen to be espousing at a particular time, for whatever reason. I don't think they are an accurate reflection of the truth that God wanted to impart to us, for I have found out from the divine world that God is love, and that we should hold no fear of him. God heals where man condemns in his name. God gives us simplicity to live by. Man corrupts this, with leaders playing mighty roles, and people then having to live accordingly. The greatest leader lived according to the will of God – simply. So how are we to follow these so-called leaders, when in our hearts we know many of them to be spiritually and morally corrupt?

Motular: Live by doing good for others; respect all life. Your deeds must be based on love, and they must come from your heart and soul. Always stand by your views; that is what makes someone the person they are.

Joseph: Can you tell me, Motular, why it is that people fear death so much – even some people who say they don't believe in a life after this one?

Motular: There are two main reasons. Firstly, ever since the human race began, leaders have instilled this fear in people to keep a spiritual stranglehold over them – to keep them "in order" for one reason or another. Secondly, people are well aware deep in their hearts that there is something beyond their world, and they may fear they have not fulfilled what they came to Earth for.

Your leaders have always taught that God is vengeful and full of wrath, and that you will burn in hell if you haven't lived your life to his glory in some way or other. What nonsense you have been spun. If this were so, we would never learn how to rise to any spiritual heights at all. Do you really think that God, whose love is beyond any mortal understanding, would destroy his creation? How could a father treat his children in such a way? Would you wish something so dreadful on your children, no matter what they had done? No! Of course not!

God's love is so powerful, so pure, so supreme and so majestic that it is beyond the comprehension even of those of us who are here in the divine world. Even from this vantage point, we can only marvel at the immensity of his goodwill to all life, and the immensity of his forgiveness.

Fear of God is a wrong signal to send to the young of your world, with its connotations of dread. The signal your leaders should be sending instead is one of love and respect for all life. Your leaders should be teaching the young that what they can see and what happens on earth is only one part of their lives, and that God is a part of everything that happens to them. Your young people need to learn to believe that God is a part of them as much as any earthly parent is – he is not just an invisible force. People's deep feelings for God are in fact deep feelings of wonder at his love for them. The right words are not *fear of God*. The right words are *wondrous awe*. When people know God is there for them, death will no longer be something frightening, but rather something to hold proud to, when they have fulfilled what they were meant to fulfil in their lives. Remember that not all fulfil their destiny, but God is a deity of rewards. All that is good in life does not go unnoticed. By the same token, you will answer to God for the evils you have done, but do not expect to go to a great fire. Do expect that you will be fully aware of your shame, and that you will have to work towards putting things right in whichever way may be determined for you. No victim is ever overlooked. All are helped to deal with their loss, in a way that Earth people do not understand.

But do not think that evil goes unpunished. It is dealt with in a way that goes far beyond human understanding, and far deeper than a life sentence in a prison, because those who have wrought evil have to repay their debts, and develop in ways that even those with much spiritual knowledge find staggering.

Joseph: Thank you, Thelma, Edward and Motular, for explaining all these things. I am very grateful to all of you.

Motular: You are most welcome, Joseph, and I don't mind telling you, we've all found this meeting far easier than Chou intimated. He said you're far too businesslike, and sometimes when he's talking with you he feels like he's at a job interview. But we all know Chou so well, we understand it's just his sense of humour.

Joseph: You see what I have to put up with!

Who Are We?

*What a huge question. I hardly know where to be-
gin… What I would like to ask, really, is: Are we all
completely of Earth? Or are we somehow a part of
extraterrestrial life? Are all of us who are born on Earth
as human beings actually Earth souls, or do some of
us come from other worlds? Do some of us come from
planets, or even dimensions, that are utterly different
from Earth? (I've met some people in my life who definitely seemed to be from another planet, but, um… I'll
stop there…)*

Joseph: Could anybody help me?

*I hope I'm not being presumptuous asking for Spirit
to come and answer my questions. But I so love it when
they come and speak with me, not only for the knowledge they give, but also for their wonderful compan-
ionship.*

Friends: Here we are!

Joseph: Oh!

There are three spirits here, and they are all chiming in together – it would be no mean feat to put the right name to every sentence they speak. I will just refer to them all as 'Friends'.

Friends: It's the three musketeers here.

Joseph: Pardon me, but...

Friends: No, you silly! We're just joking with you! The three of us are always together.

Joseph: Well I can see you're not the three wise monkeys!

Friends: We're called Matthew – that's me – and Mickey and Moss. We've come to answer your question.

Joseph: It is quite a big question – I'll try and break it down into a few different parts.

Friends: OK.

Joseph: Can you please tell me if Earth, at the beginning of its development, was visited by – shall I say – alien life?

Friends: Yes, it was. Not all the universe developed at the same time. By the time Earth was ready to receive life, life already existed on some other planets at quite an advanced level.

Joseph: What about the story of Adam and Eve? Some people of my time think they were from an alien world.

Friends: Naughty, naughty, Joseph…

Joseph: I was only asking your opinion! Of course I believe in the creation of mankind. But I'm not sure I entirely believe the story of Adam and Eve – it is from so far back in history, and it has been passed down through the ages innumerable times. On the other hand, most good stories have some basis in fact, and knowing God and the way he is so good towards life, I can well believe that something like that might have taken place.

As to whether alien life met people of Earth in times gone by, there are plenty of strange meetings described in the Bible. I'm thinking of Ezekiel and his experiences, the prophet Elijah who went up into heaven in a chariot, and others too numerous to mention. I believe that the Earth people of the time assumed their visitors were angels, as they had no knowledge of anything else. But there are clear differences in the Bible when it is an angel who appears; the whole experience is different.

Friends: History does record strange visitors from the sky. And they are certainly seen even to this day in your world, so you can be sure you are not alone in the universe.

Joseph: Can Earth souls be reborn in other worlds? And can the souls of extraterrestrials be born on Earth?

Friends: Some integration does take place, but it takes a very developed soul to be able to cope with this.

Joseph: Does alien life interbreed with human life? There are stories of this in our myths and legends; some of the great civilisations of the past believed that their kings were the descendants of gods from the skies.

Friends: Where there is intelligent life there will always be interbreeding, in the same way as different cultures on Earth interbreed now.

Joseph: Surely this must bring about tremendous problems?

Friends: Only at this point in the Earth's history. As more and more forms of life become aware of Earth's readiness to integrate, then more beings from other worlds will make their presence known to the world.

Joseph: Interesting… That brings me to another question: When that time comes, and children are born from Earth's people interbreeding with other life forms, will a new type of soul appear?

Friends: No. Souls, as you know, have the capacity to learn great mountains of knowledge, so they will just adjust to their new environment. But they will also be endowed with superintelligence, because they will have the knowledge within them of two distinct worlds.

Joseph: Three. The wisdom of the spirit world will give them yet another source of knowledge to draw on.

Friends: Yes, that is true. And they may be reborn many times, in a variety of different worlds. This may help to bring greater stability to all in an everchanging universe.

Joseph: Is there other life close to our world, just a "bus ride" away in terms of distance and travelling time?

Friends: At one stage in its history, the red planet, Mars, had life forms on it. But to visit the kind of life you mean – an independent, thinking life form – you would have needed to book your bus trip before you were even born. You would have to travel all your living days, and way past your earthly life span.

Joseph: The mind boggles. Do you think that in

the near future we'll be able to travel to other solar systems, the way we see on some of our TV programmes, like *Star Trek*?

Friends: One day human beings will travel the universe, although this will not happen in the near future. But you have made a good start, for you have already reached out by travelling to the moon, and sending unmanned craft to different parts of your solar system.

Joseph: Yes, but this raises other questions. We spend billions on these projects – money which I often feel we should be spending on the poor and the needy in our society instead.

Friends: Of course it is absolutely right that societies should look after these people in every way possible. But as you well know, Joseph, there is plenty on Earth to go round – it is only the *will* to ensure this happens that is lacking at the moment. Indeed it is true that some of your leaders are spiritually and morally dead, caring only for their own puny needs. But space exploration is not wasted money, in the sense that these projects are a part of the Earth's future.

Joseph: The allocation of resources is not the only moral issue. History has proved that the people of

Earth are very warlike – always ready to invade other people's lands as and when it suits them. As you say, some of Earth's leaders are dead to the needs of others, and I can't foresee they will be any different in the future. Surely this could bring about absolute disaster.

Friends: But Joseph, the people of Earth will not be the superior intellects. By the time human beings have gained any standing in the pecking order, they will hopefully have learned to live by the laws of peace.

Joseph: Amen to that! And thank you all so much. I have so enjoyed your visit! God bless you. The old body is growing weary once again. But if it weren't for that, I'm sure I could go on talking all night.

Friends: One of us – and I'm not saying who – just said you *have* gone on all night!

Hierarchy, Wealth, Fame

In the Middle Ages, if you were born poor, you stayed poor, and if you were born rich, there was a very good chance you would hang on to your money. Rich people would buy "indulgences" from the church in an attempt to absolve themselves of sin; the poor could not even contemplate this. Moving up the social ladder was all but impossible. Everything was geared to people knowing their place, and woe betide them if they tried to step beyond that. In modern times it is possible for some people, given the right circumstances, to rise in the ranks financially, but even then, "new money" is often looked down on by "old money". There is no society on Earth that is without a hierarchy. So I wonder, is there a hierarchy in the spirit world?

Jack: Hello, it's Jack here! I've come to answer your question.

Joseph: Jack! Hello! It's so nice to see you and talk with you again.

Jack lived in the sixteenth century. He was what in Britain we would call a barrow boy. He is such a cheerful soul. He has told me he has no wish to be reborn. He says that one day he will need to return to fulfil some part of his destiny, but he has no wish to speed the process up.

Jack: Yes, there is a hierarchy in the spirit world, but not in the way that people of your world would understand it, for as you have said, they are too wrapped up in their own importance. The hierarchy of the spirit world is based on love – unselfish love – the love that asks for nothing and gives everything. That is the law of God.

Souls who have reached the rank of angel and above have got there through their own spirituality and their understanding of the laws of God. They serve in sheer joy. When they are serving other people, throughout the divine world and throughout the universe, their happiness is beyond human understanding. They never give themselves airs and graces. They are fully aware of God's majesty, and when they are sent by him to people, they are true to their Creator's call by appearing in such a way that humans know they are from God. Look to the greatest soul in the history of the world. If earthly social rank is of any importance, why was the Son of God born in such humble circumstances? The ranks of the divine world are built on love.

Joseph: In your experience, Jack, do souls who have lived on earth ever rise to this level of love?

Jack: Yes, indeed they do, for example many of those whom people call saints. And there are plenty of people thought of as very ordinary in your world who rise to magnificent spiritual heights because of their great godliness. You can rest assured that in heaven it is known who the real servers are – they are easily distinguishable from those who deceive people with their lukewarm giving.

Joseph: So beware, leaders. Life on Earth may seem long. But in terms of how long your soul lives for – eternally – life is very, very brief. I take this as a lesson to myself, too.

Does God uphold any particular rank on Earth?

Jack: He only upholds those individuals who are deemed to be of good heart and who act for the sake of mankind, for as you know, more often than not, rank is oppressive to people and stunts their natural and spiritual growth. Titles given to people on Earth to distinguish them from others hold no sway in the divine world; they are left behind when the soul returns. Instead, people are recognised by their deeds.

Joseph: Could I ask you a different question, please?

Jack: Certainly.

Joseph: Much is said and done in God's name. Nations and organisations go to war and inflict great cruelty while claiming their actions are the will of God. How do you think God perceives this?

Jack: God is very loving and forgiving, but as you know, from time to time he steps in and responds. Then he shows his majesty to the world in some startling display. Also, there are people like yourself who speak to us, who have a responsibility to alert the world to its rights and wrongs.

Joseph: People like me are usually looked upon as some kind of nutcase. The leaders of the established religions would never give any credence to someone like me, or my peers.

Jack: Since when have you been concerned about what people think of you, Joseph? Like all people who serve as you do, you have a spiritual overcoat that you wear against bigotry. Nothing ever changes unless there are people who will stand up and say it as it is. Remember, the Master died so that the truth would be heard. Many wars have been fought so that people may say what they wish to. Truth is the greatest hope that the human race has.

Joseph: It is said in the Bible that it is easier for a camel to go through the eye of a needle than for a rich man to enter into the kingdom of God. Is that entirely true?

Jack: Not in the sense that there are people who do great good with their wealth. Usually you will find that it's the poor who have become wealthy somehow or other who do the most good. Established wealth generally just stays that way. You only need to look around your home country to see how true that is.

Joseph: In the unlikely event that I were to become wealthy one day, (is that laughter I hear in the background?) how should I dispose of my hypothetical wealth?

Jack: You would need to be vastly wealthy to do all the things that you want to do, and you will not attain that status. You should help your nearest and dearest, follow through with the plan that has been mapped out for you, and remember to give wherever the need is the greatest, within your awareness.

Joseph: One of my problems is that I am very well aware of the state of the world.

Jack: So move yourself to do something about it, then. It often takes only one person to do a fantastic amount of good. Mother Teresa is a shining example. She was very poor, but she gave hope to millions of souls in one way or another. We wish that leaders of nations would learn from her life's experience. Monetary riches are not always the answer. But the richness that flows from giving of oneself is.

Joseph: To round off everything we've been talking about, could I ask you one more question, please? Are there many disillusioned souls among the kings and queens, popes and bishops, and political leaders of the world, who have not made the spiritual jump because of their sense of self-importance, but who nonetheless expect to stay in their positions?

Jack: Yes. There are very many who have failed to do what they should have done in their roles, often even at the most basic levels of their responsibility. How can they expect to make headway with this kind of attitude? Position always brings responsibility.

Joseph: I know that fame on Earth is of little or no importance, unless it is for a particular purpose. Over the years, many souls who were famous in my world for one reason or another have come to talk with me. They don't only talk with me, of course; there are plenty of other people who are lucky enough to be able to speak with those from the divine world. But I rarely mention these conversations to anyone else. Basically I think it is because so many people say that such-and-such a famous person has come to talk with them – so much so that it gives the impression that every other person in the spirit world who contacts someone on earth has been famous. Either that, or their guides are Native American chiefs or little Chinese men. (Sorry, Chou, no offence intended!) Anyway, Chou never claims to be a famous soul, although to me he goes far beyond that. And Titus is so humble and goes so far back in history that he is not really thought of as famous in today's world. I have, as I often do, gone round the houses to ask my question. What I am wondering about is this: Am I being unjust by not giving souls who were once famous the chance of being heard again by people on Earth?

Jack: That depends on the reasons why they want to communicate. They are souls like the rest of us. If you find that you can be of service to them, and they can be of service to the world, then please go ahead.

I have to say I'm glad, though, that you're not one of those people who would capitalise on your meetings with the so-called famous.

Now, Joseph, some time ago you said you were rounding off our chat together, so let's call our pleasant meeting to an end.

Joseph: I'm sorry, Jack. I was absolutely engrossed. You're always so wise and full of knowledge that I lose track of time. Many, many thanks.

Guardian Angels

A guardian angel is a soul in the divine world who has attained the highest levels of purity and gentleness, and who is then given by God the responsibility of ministering to an earthly person. A guardian angel may also be called a divine messenger, a ministering spirit, or a guide.

Joseph: Please may I speak to someone who knows about this subject?

Antoninus: Hello, my name is Antoninus. And I am a guide.

Joseph: Hello, Antoninus! I'm so thrilled you've come to speak with me. You have quite an uncommon name.

Antoninus: Yes, I do. But I'm not Antoninus the Roman emperor. I hope you're not disappointed.

Joseph: On the contrary, Antoninus! I'm just

always amazed at the kindness of the spirit world in coming to answer my sometimes infantile questions.

Antoninus: Perhaps I should start by explaining how we come to be guides. I will use the term "guide", as it is the one you are most familiar with.

A soul who wishes to become a guide goes on a course of training that not only deals with every aspect of human nature, but also teaches an understanding of the deep spiritual nature of all life. It is a long and rigorous training. No one becomes a guide unless they master what this course teaches. But the most important thing of all is to learn to give unselfish love.

Joseph: Can ordinary people become guides?

Antoninus: Of course they can! Why ever not? I would say the great majority of guides come into this category, if there is such a thing as an "ordinary person".

Joseph: We accept the role that our guides play as a basic part of our lives.

Antoninus: Do you, indeed?!

Joseph: I'm sorry, Antoninus, I didn't mean it to sound that way. What I meant was that because God gives us his love and help, and the guides work to that end too, they become a part of us, and our experience of life.

Could I ask you if guides have specific tasks to perform at different times in our lives?

Antoninus: Yes, we do have certain specific tasks to perform. We also try to help our charges understand how to live their lives better. And another part of our responsibility is to help them understand they must work towards their destiny.

Joseph: With the greatest of respect to you and your colleagues, there must be a lot of very disappointed guides floating around heaven. I suspect my own guides come into this category.

Antoninus: Actually, there are not as many as you might think. In people's lives there is always some success, and what the world may think of as failure, we may deem otherwise. No one I know leads a perfect life while on earth... apart from the holy ones, and they are few indeed.

Joseph: How do guides feel when their charges commit acts such as murder, or become Hitlers?

Antoninus: As you well know, we are there to help and advise our charges – *not* to take over their lives and souls. There is free will for all, good or bad. The good are easy to guide; with the less good it takes longer, but we never give up on a soul, even if we have to seek out more help than we are able to give ourselves. But this happens only rarely.

Joseph: Some people see their guide at certain times in their life, whereas others never do. Why is this?

Antoninus: There are many thousands of reasons – too many to go into – but some see their guide when they are in a time of great need. Others find that at a certain moment in their life their spiritual channel opens, for reasons not obvious even to themselves.

Joseph: In my life, Antoninus, I have met many wonderful people who would dearly love to see or speak to their guide, but they never have. Others I have met have been… well… not the nicest people (I'm sorry if I appear to be making judgements against my fellow human beings; I'll call it making observations…) and yet they have seen and do see Spirit.

Antoninus: Once again, there could be any number of different reasons for this. There must have been factors at play that were not obvious to yourself or others. As you are aware, Spirit, and guides in particular, never do anything unless there is a very good reason for it.

Joseph: Do many souls wish to become guides?

Antoninus: Yes, very many. And many want to

be helpers to guides, as this is an excellent training ground too, which allows them to fulfil many criteria at once. For example, if they wish to be reborn, they will return to Earth with a greater knowledge than they had before, and their learning will benefit many people. Then there are other souls who aspire to go on and become experts in a particular area of learning. They usually stay on this side of life and keep working towards their goal.

Joseph: May I ask you, Antoninus, what your aim is? Would you like to continue being a guide, or are you interested in doing something else?

Antoninus: I am very, very happy being a guide, but there are other things I would like to do too, so when the time is right I will move on to fulfil other parts of my destiny.

Joseph: Might I be permitted to know who you are guide to at the moment?

Antoninus: It is to a very nice person who you don't yet know, but who you will meet when the time is right. That's why I have made myself known to you now.

Joseph: Thank you, Antoninus, for all your help and understanding. I look forward to seeing you in the future. God bless.

Creatures Mythical
and Unexplained

Eleven years have passed since Chou first helped me make up some notes about these beings. Now that I'm writing again, I'm asking Chou for some more help… actually I'm hoping he will help me complete this chapter.

Joseph: Hello, Chou, how are you, my friend?

Chou: Oh! I see! It's creepy time. My "friend" indeed!

Joseph: Well, yes, I am creeping. But only a tiny bit, because I am happy to see you and talk with you again.

Chou: OK, fire away then…

Joseph: Are there such people as leprechauns?

Chou: Long ago in the mists of time when people were much smaller than they are now, there were people who were born very small indeed. Today you would call them dwarfs or little people. But today's dwarfs are tall compared to the size dwarfs were way back then. They were often cast out of society because they were so different from the rest. In order to survive, they became herbalists, and they also performed all sorts of magic on people. Today you would call it medicine, but in those days it was a different story. As time passed, these little people became associated with magical ways, and in some respects became something to be feared.

Joseph: Why were they born so small?

Chou: It was partly to do with poor diets at the time and partly to do with genetics. As time marched on, leprechauns became a part of legend.

Joseph: Could you tell me something about gnomes, please?

Chou: Certainly. Human beings think of gnomes as sprites who live in the inner part of the earth and guard its treasures.

Joseph: Yes, but do they really live there, or just in people's imaginations?

Chou: History has intermixed with folk tales. And the folk tales have got mixed up too; as different cultures have interbred, aspects of their different legends and stories have become intertwined.

Gnomes were unusually small people who were labelled as freaks by unkind people. So they tended to hide themselves away from society and live in places like woodlands and caves. The concept of the "gnome" was a way of thinking of people who were outcasts; they were not a separate species. So yes, gnomes existed, but not in the way you think of them today.

Joseph: And what are goblins, then?

Chou: They are frightful sprites. They can also be called bogeymen.

Joseph: When I was a child, my brothers and sisters used to say that if you misbehaved, a goblin would come and get you. My eldest brother says I was weird because when he told me that a goblin would take me away, I would giggle and get excited, and say I couldn't wait for it to arrive.

Chou: I remember that, and the reasons why.

Joseph: Even to this day, I still like the idea of little goblins, but I have never met one, and when I ask other people if they have, the answer is always no.

Chou: You're not likely to, either. They only exist in the same way as leprechauns and gnomes – in myth and legend.

Joseph: That's a shame. I wanted there to be goblins!

Chou: As your guide, I must say I wonder about you sometimes. Maybe I drew the short straw!

Joseph: What about fairies?

Chou: What you must remember is that there are many things in heaven and on earth that are not necessarily shown to human beings. It would be a very convoluted exercise to try to explain about fairies in a way that would make sense to you. It would take another book. Not everything in your world can always be explained, and fairies come into this category.

Joseph: So do fairies exist or not?

Chou: I don't believe you have been listening! I have just been telling you that there are many things in heaven and on earth that are not shown to humans! Perhaps some other time we can discuss the subject more fully.

Joseph: OK then, Chou, I'll book that one in for a later date. In the meantime, could you please tell me what a harpy is?

Chou: Harpies are rapacious monsters that are part-woman and part-bird. They go back to prehistory, to the time when dinosaurs walked the earth and flying reptiles known as pterodactyls took to the skies. These creatures linked in with the terrors of the human mind, so over time they became something to fear in the same way that dragons did.

Joseph: Have they ever existed?

Chou: Once again, not in the way that societies perceive them. As with most myths and legends, there is certainly an element of truth, but over the ages many changes have been made to suit different people and different times.

There is a real dragon, which is a kind of lizard. But the fabled, winged kind of dragon does not exist.

Joseph: One day as I was crossing a bridge I saw a green globe floating in the air. I have asked you before what it was, and you have never told me, so I suppose you're not going to now either…

Chou: It was to do with extraterrestrials, and my lips are now sealed on the subject.

Joseph: May I ask you about some of the strange creatures in the spirit world, then?

Chou: At some of the lower levels there are forms of life that make me shiver a little, but only because they are so different from the life forms I'm used to.

Joseph: In all the years I've known you, Chou, this is the first time I've heard you say something that someone might think was even slightly unpleasant! Wow!

Chou: Well, Joseph, they say you learn something

new every day. In our wonderful pools of history we cover every aspect of the universe and the divine world. There are sights that would boggle the mind.

Joseph: I would love to be let loose in the pools of history. Just think, Chou, what wonderful books I could write!

Chou: Stick to what you know.

Truths and Myths of the Bible

It is absolutely not my intention to denigrate the Good Book, but I have felt the need to ask Spirit many questions about the Bible over the years. I have wanted to know what is fact, and where – shall we say – poetic licence has been taken. I have also wanted to find out more about some of the most wonderful events in human history – nowhere are these more apparent than in the Bible.

The questions that follow were put to Spirit over a period of years – not just in one sitting. In transcribing the answers I shall simply refer to the different speakers as Spirit, in accordance with their wishes.

First conversation:

Joseph: In Genesis, the serpent tested Adam and Eve in the Garden of Eden. But I can't help wondering whether the story was related in the way it was to put the misgivings of mankind onto someone else's shoulders, thereby freeing people from their own responsibilities.

Spirit: Because the written word did not exist at that time, events were passed down the ages in the form of stories. In this way, of course, things got added, and other things got taken away.

Eventually the written word came into being, and it became a kind of permanent record. But as written texts started to be produced, artistic licence began to come into play. Moreover, every time a story was translated into another language, its meanings were altered. Nonetheless, many, many events are record-ed in the Bible, which, whether they lend themselves easily to human understanding or not, are still true.

The early storytellers were well aware that there had been a Creation, and that some power must have designed and formed things. They also knew full well that on Earth they were the highest form of life. Logic told them that the beginning for them was not the same as it had been for other life forms. Certainly the early storytellers were thinking beings, and they reached the conclusion that everything that was wrong in the world was not their fault, but someone else's – in the process freeing themselves from responsibility…

Of course a power that is evil exists too; and I still say that the responsibility rests with the individual to reject evil, just as the responsibility rests with the individual to accept good. The power of good is the ruling power, so instead of passing responsibility for one's actions over to a power of evil, as has been done in the past, people must always ask themselves: Why accept that evil has a place within oneself?

Joseph: I hear what you are saying, but surely there is another issue going on here too. The powers that a soul living on Earth is aware of are the power of good and the power of evil. Mankind has lived so long with both. But different cultures see things in different ways: what is evil in one culture is not evil in another. With the greatest of respect, if mankind gives credence to evil – and it does – is this really our individual responsibility?

Spirit: Please listen more closely to what I have said, Joseph. You have a responsibility to yourself to develop your soul. No power, however evil, should ever have the kind of hold over you whereby you would lay the responsibility for your actions at its door. If you were to do so, you would be saying you are willing for that power to have a hold over your life.

Joseph: I do understand what you are saying to me, my friend, but with the greatest of respect to you, I live in this world, and I see the evil that humans inflict on each other. Very often it is the innocent who suffer the most for it. In my own life, too, I fall victim every day to some degree – to a minor degree, I hope – to this thing we call evil. For instance, there are times when I've had a hard day and the telephone rings late at night and someone needs my help. I sometimes feel like saying, "Go and take a walk!" Is that bad and selfish of me? In view of what you have said, it seems an evil thing to think. On the other hand, I have also been told by Spirit that God doesn't expect us to be perfect. Please don't think I am challenging you, for you make so much sense, but I feel I would be a hypocrite not to air my views.

Spirit: Of course you must speak your truth – that is what the divine world stands for. The scenario from your own life that you have just described is not an example of evil.

In all situations you need to look at your motives, and respond in the way that best suits your spiritual development. When everyone does that, the world will be a much better place.

Joseph: What you are saying, my friend, is that it

is up to each soul to reject evil and its power, and by doing so, we will eliminate the power that evil has in the world.

Spirit: Yes.

Joseph: You have answered my question about the serpent in the garden! Thank you so much for your patience with me. God bless you.

Second conversation:

Joseph: One of the most magnificent events in the Bible is the Exodus, and the lead-up to it. It fires my hope for mankind, inasmuch as we too might have a great push and then a spiritual move forward.

Spirit: Where would like me to start?

Joseph: The first thing I would like to know is: Did it really happen? I believe that it did, but just because I want to believe in it doesn't make it fact.

Spirit: It happened as surely as you're sitting on that chair.

Joseph: Thank you.

Spirit: The whole nation was made ready, then the journey began. To me it was the greatest miracle, on the grandest scale, in the history of the human race.

Joseph: I can't get the epic film version out of my mind: Charlton Heston with flowing beard and outstretched arms, carrying a staff… It all fires the blood in such a romantic way that I think I might have put a pair of rose-coloured glasses on. Was it really anything like that?

Spirit: You have a watered-down version of the actual event, for Moses was a fine figure of a man. The actor who portrayed him was very puny compared to Moses. Remember, Moses got a whole nation to follow him. Through his faith in God, Moses got a pharaoh to bend to God's will. The nation dwelt many years under the wise rule of Moses.

Joseph: Did Moses stutter? We are led to believe he had a stutter and his brother Aaron did all the talking for him.

Spirit: No, he did not. He had a fine strong voice. Anyone who was on the receiving end of one of his outbursts will tell you he had no stutter.

Joseph: It always saddens me to think that Moses never went into the Promised Land. Was that a part of his destiny?

Spirit: Moses fulfilled his promise by doing God's will. He was not interested in what he wanted for himself, for in the deepest part of his heart he had what he wanted, and that was to serve God.

Joseph: Moses is even more of a hero to me now

that I know something about him as a person.

Would you mind if we backtracked a little? How did Moses part the sea to let the people cross to the other side?

Spirit: It was God who parted the sea. It was the most wondrous sight. Moses stood on high ground and encouraged the people to cross to the other side. Words cannot express the marvel of it.

Joseph: Thank you so much. I have so enjoyed speaking with you. God bless you, my friend.

Spirit: You are most welcome, Joseph. We will talk again soon. Peace to your family.

Third conversation:

Joseph: I would like to ask you about what for me is the most exciting time in the history of the world – the life of the Lord Jesus. If I could have one wish, it would be to travel through time to the life of the Master.

Spirit: The Master Jesus was full of grace and the spirit of God, as he still is now, of course. But I can tell you, the image the world has of Jesus as meek and mild has very little to do with the reality of his life. Meek and mild is only an accurate description of Christ in the sense of the gentleness and kindness of his divine spirituality. You will recall that the Master

Jesus lived at a time of great upheaval. The Romans were in occupation, and the leaders of the religions were fighting tooth and nail to hang on to their own little domains. (Joseph, do you recognise the parallel with your world today?) So you will realise that the Master Jesus was a very strong person in every sense of the word. It would have been impossible to live the life that the Master Jesus did and be of a fragile demeanour. I assure you he could rough it with the best.

The disciples were hardy men too. Some had been fishermen, and knew that their hands were not only for eating and working, but also for defending themselves with. Do you really think that sort of person would have followed a physically weak character? Basically they lived on the road and met all kinds of people, and the Master Jesus lived life to the full.

One of the many amazing things about the Master Jesus was his skill at communicating. He had – and still has – the ability to speak at every level, to all different kinds of people, and to be understood by all. And today every nation loves and respects his message.

Joseph: From what friends in the spirit world have told me over the years, the Master was also a very humble person. I would have loved to see him working his miracles.

Spirit: There was never any flash-bang-wallop kind of miracle with the Master; everything was always done in a very natural way, with a laying on of his hands, a word here, a touch there. The Master Jesus was always very thankful for any tiny thing that people did for him, but he also had great strength when it was called for. No one ever put one over him in his life. The outcome was only different when it was the will of God that it should be so. Your leaders today should follow his examples, and they would never need to have any worries about being re-elected.

Joseph: Thank you all so much for speaking to me. I'm so lucky to have such wonderful friends in the divine world. You make writing this book so much fun!

Does God Really
Care about the World?

I asked one evening if I could speak to someone who knows what God thinks about the way human beings treat each other.

The person who came and spoke to me had been a white friar. He told me that had spent most of his life in a forest in Shropshire, and that while he was living there he had begun to understand what God really wanted of him. Since his promotion to the higher side of life, he has realised that while in the physical world, he was indeed following his destiny. Now he works from the other side of life to help groups who seek to contain the destruction of the life that God has put on Earth.

Joseph: May I ask your name, please?

Sebastian: I am Sebastian.

Joseph: Hello, Sebastian. It is a pleasure to meet you, and thank you for coming to help me with my questions and answers. Some of my questions may surprise you; you may think, "Why is he asking this when he already knows…" I feel in my heart that I already know the answers to what I am about to ask you, but I want to make sure my understandings are absolutely correct. Certainly the divine world has taught me I must always check the facts.

Sebastian: That is very wise of you, Joseph, because even when people have the very best of intentions and motives in life, it does not necessarily mean their ideas are facts; only facts are facts.

Joseph: Please do not mistake my belief in the power of God when I ask if he really cares about what goes on in the world. I am fully aware of his love for all his children, good or bad. To my mind, and in my experience, that is not in question. But I do wonder at some of the things I see happening. For instance, I look around the world and see leaders of nations who are an abomination, who bring incalculable suffering and destruction to people. Why do these despots rise to such great power so they can then wreak havoc on the innocent?

Sebastian: I accept what you are saying, Joseph, but you know and understand about free will. Despots can only rise to such heights of power if people allow them to. You know that if people find a situation unacceptable and they stand together, they have the power to change events. It is not a question of whether God cares – of course he does. But the power is in the hands of people. You are not puppets of God. You are spiritual and freethinking souls, and you have choices.

Joseph: Please excuse my insistence, Sebastian, but that is not always the case. People in many countries try very hard to free themselves from all sorts of tyrannies, only to end up in a worse situation. Millions have even lost their lives trying to use the power of their freedom of choice.

Sebastian: Look through the history of the world and you will find that all the powers that oppress are brought to their knees by the power of good in people. Mighty empires fall because of their injustices. Even between individuals, true justice prevails.

Joseph: Are you saying that wrongs are always put right at some point, whatever the circumstances? Or am I misinterpreting you?

Sebastian: The justice of God is that all is made right in the fullness of time through the development of the soul. God is always aware of injustices. You only have to leaf through the Holy Book to realise this. God, whose every act is of unconditional love, ensures that the offending soul is made aware of its sins and is encouraged to put its wrongs right.

Joseph: Well what about Hitler and his cronies, and all the other despots? How will they ever make amends for the injustices they have wrought on many millions of people?

Sebastian: By the power of right, they will be aware for all time of the wrongs they have committed. And through the power of God, they will work to return some of the rights they have taken away from souls. But in the meantime, God, with his great love, heals the souls who have suffered.

Joseph: I can well believe that God heals with his great love, but I think I must be a long way away from a complete understanding of what you are saying to me. Undoubtedly I have a lot of growing to do. But I feel it is too easy for these despots, and that innocent victims need to see justice done to help their own souls go forward in spiritual growth.

Sebastian: Of course justice must be seen to be done. And faith is essential – knowing and trusting that God rights all wrongs. He does not right them in a way that mankind would comprehend, but rather by the law of God, which goes far beyond the understanding of all mortals, and to some extent even surpasses the understanding of angels.

Joseph: Well, thank you, Sebastian. May I please go on to another subject?

Sebastian: I am happy to help you in your quest for answers.

Joseph: We know that God's power is everywhere at all times, and we can often feel his energy in people's good actions. But many times I have asked Spirit if they have seen something of God that is tangible.

Sebastian: As you well know, Joseph, in our world we are more aware of the power of God than you are in yours. His energy moves like a great wind across the heavenly kingdoms. We feel him everywhere we are. This brings us great comfort, and it also inspires us to strive harder to reach our goals.

The more highly evolved a soul is, the more he or she feels almost the solidness of God. Those archangels who are so evolved that they reach into the very presence of God tell those of us who are yet to reach such wonderful states of spiritual development that God appears as a light far brighter than all the suns put together. And yet this is still only a part of God. They tell us that they do not see his face in the way that people on Earth would think of it, but his wonderful love pours forth like a great ocean.

Joseph: It brings a warm glow to me to know that God is also in everything we try to do for the human race.

Sebastian: He is indeed.

Joseph: Do the archangels tell you anything about what God portrays of his own feelings? We always hear of his great love for all of creation and his very giving nature, but we never hear anything about what his own feelings are on different matters. Or am I being naïve, using human criteria to ask a question about God?

Sebastian: I believe that God would appreciate your asking such a question. It is only right that children should ask how their father is, even when he is the Father Creator.

The archangels tell us that God only ever shows love for all of his creation, that his joy is in all things, and that it brings him great happiness when a soul becomes aware of its spiritual self. We know also that he is happy when souls ask him for the help that they may need. Of course God's help comes in many forms, and rarely as we would expect it, for God helps the soul for many ages ahead, far beyond the immediate situation for which help is being sought.

Joseph: May I ask a difficult question of you? What do you think God thinks of the princes and overseers of his church? I am referring to all the religions and faiths, and to denominations of every kind.

Sebastian: We know in our world that God is very unhappy to see how people's hopes are treated by the houses that are raised in his name. It is known that the leaders of many churches have lost their way, and only see through blinkers. They should return to the good that originally established the houses of God. They should listen to Jesus Christ, and to the other great spiritual souls. Only in this way will God ever respect the leaders.

But there is a ray of light, because there are lay people, priests at grass-roots level, and other souls who so want the world to recognise the love of God, who are working to bring back hope to people. We are happy that many of the young see new hope in organisations that show spiritual awareness, offer guidance, and encourage free thinking towards positive results. By their actions, they show the houses of God that the princes of the churches must shed the trappings of gold and silver, and hold out the hand and heart of true ministry. They must bring back true meaning to their office: love through action.

Then God will be a happy creator.

Joseph: Why do you think God has arranged things in the world in the way that he has? Are things very different in the divine realms?

Sebastian: I do understand what you mean by your question, and I am aware you do not imply any criticism of the Creator. It would take many books to answer your question in full, so I will condense the history of creation into a few paragraphs.

First God created the universe, then he allowed its continued development by means of an organised evolution in accordance with the blueprint he had created for this purpose.

We are well aware of your scientists' differing views, which are absolutely no problem, for that is the point they have reached, for the moment, on the long path of progress that allows a species to develop.

As far as the human race is concerned, plenty of events have taken place on Earth that God is not too happy with, but as I explained to you earlier, he is a loving and patient God. He does not expect the world to start at school one day and graduate the next. That is why from time to time he sends great teachers to help students on the earthly plane to advance. To move towards their spirituality, as we call it. So all in all, everything is proceeding according to God's master plan. Like all great plans, God's plan for the world takes time to come to fruition.

The divine world is very different in its awareness of its spirituality. We are not embodied as earthly souls are, so we have certain freedoms that you cannot have at this time. We are far more aware of the majesty of God's works, but then that is as it should be.

Joseph: Sebastian, with the greatest of respect, you would make a wonderful politician. You say much, but very little to answer my question. Ha ha! Could you please teach me this skill?

Sebastian: Well Joseph, your guide tells me you are the greatest waffler in the business, and I can only explain as well as the listener understands.

Joseph: I stand corrected. It is my little joke, Sebastian.

Sebastian: Mine too.

Joseph: If I dare, may I ask another question?

Sebastian: Please do.

Joseph: Do you see our Lord Jesus in the divine world? If possible, rather than saying what he is doing for the world, could you please tell me something about how he likes to spend his own personal time?

Sebastian: Yes, we do see him, and he is still very approachable, just as he was when he was on Earth. As far as I understand, it is not only his work but also his play and pleasure to travel everywhere in God's creation and serve.

Joseph: May I ask one last question, please?

Sebastian: Yes.

Joseph: Is God aware of every blade of grass that grows and every sparrow that flies? I want to place God in his rightful position in the hearts of people as the true working Father that I know him to be. I want to do away with the erroneous ideas many of us have grown up with – either about him being harsh and punishing, or being a creator who sits somewhere watching over us and planning what he will do if we step out of line, or even being the God of the floating clouds, with dreamy angels fluttering around him playing harps all day long. I believe he would want us to see him as we see a loving parent – kind, full of fun and praise, a little bit mystical, frowning when our actions are wrong, and guiding us when we need to be guided (which, it seems, we always do). After all, God built the concept of parenthood into us. I feel this is how we should know him. If God really knows every blade of grass that grows and every sparrow that flies, then he will also know all our thoughts and deeds, good and bad, yet he is still there supporting us, cheering us on.

Sebastian: Yes to your very long question. God is all things to all souls. He never compromises his love and understanding, and yes, he is aware of absolutely everything, even your waffling.

Here Sebastian gives a very refined-sounding laugh.

Joseph: Thank you so much for your kindness in staying so long with me, and also for being so patient when I ask what must sometimes seem very juvenile questions.

Sebastian: It is my pleasure, Joseph. Never feel that your questions are juvenile, for you need to make your meaning clear, to Spirit and to people alike. We always say you have a great ability for explaining things to people, and putting them at their ease, because you speak with the simplicity that comes from knowing the truth of what you are saying.

I think Sebastian takes me for rather a simple soul. But he is being kind to me, in his very sophisticated way.

Mr Watts Speaks His Truth

It was an absolute delight for me on a personal level to be able to speak with Mr Watts, who is now in the spirit world.

When I was young, our mum had to work, so my brother and I were sent to a boarding school run by the local council. I was always known as a sensitive child (my brother would say a sissy).

Mr Watts was my teacher and housemaster. But he was more like an elderly uncle, really, with a worn and fleshy face. That is the best I can describe him.

I was heartbroken when he died, for he used to listen to my ramblings about Spirit, and he never poked fun at me. Now all these years later he has come to visit me in my home. The visit went like this:

I was sitting watching television, when I became aware of another presence in the room, so I turned round. Mr Watts was sitting on the chair by the door to the hallway. For a few seconds I felt delighted to see him. This quickly turned to sadness as all the memories of how I had missed him came flooding back.

Mr Watts: Hello, Joseph.

Joseph: Hello, Sir.

I was in tears.

It's so nice to see you! You look wonderful.

Mr Watts: I feel wonderful, too. It's amazing what a good rest and a new life can do for you.

Mr Watts smiled that magnificent fleshy smile of his. And I felt like a small boy again, all warm and safe.

Joseph: Please come and sit in the armchair, Sir.

I almost said "I'll put the kettle on…"

How are you doing in your world, Sir? Are you still teaching and looking after little horrors like me?

Mr Watts: No, no! I am training to be a guide. Also, I have musical leanings that I would like to develop further, God willing.

Joseph: I'm so happy for you, Sir.

Mr Watts: You know, Joseph, over the years I have always kept an eye on your career. You've not done too badly.

Joseph: Thank you, Sir.

I won't bore you with a full transcript of our

conversation; instead I'll get to the part that I hope you'll enjoy as much as I did.

Joseph: Sir, before you left this world, did you know there was another world waiting for you?

Mr Watts: There's no need to call me Sir, Joseph.

Joseph: It's because I wish to show you the same love and respect that I did as a child.

Meeting Mr Watts again was making me feel exactly like I did when I was a small boy, all over again.

Mr Watts: Right through my life on Earth, Joseph, I always believed, in a simple way, that I would meet my mother and father again.

I was moved by the thought of that wonderful elderly teacher with his childlike ways and his straightforward belief that he would see his parents again.

Joseph: And I feel sure you did meet your mother and father again.

Mr Watts: Indeed I did.

Joseph: I am so happy for you.

Could I please ask you about your… how shall I put it… the logistics of your arrival into the world of Spirit?

Mr Watts: As you well know, Joseph, before I passed I was very ill. During that time I became confused about my surroundings. Finally I drew my last breath. I felt myself floating, as if I was as light as a feather. I felt fearful, though, that I was going to land with a crash on the floor. Then suddenly I became aware that two people were holding my hands, one on either side of me. I couldn't see them, but I knew instantly that they were my mother and my father.

I was trying to be all mature and grown up, but in the presence of my wonderful childhood mentor I really did feel like a little boy all over again, now with tears of happiness in my eyes for Mr Watts and his arrival into the world of Spirit.

Mr Watts: Next I was on the ground again, and I could see who was holding my hands. Yes, it was definitely my mother and father. They smiled at me, and my mother said, "How lovely to see you again, son!" She gave me a great big hug. My father said, "Welcome home, son," and gave me a kiss on the cheek.

I was so delighted to see them that I forgot everything else. It was only when my mother said, "Look back, son, and say goodbye to your faithful old body," that I realised I had died.

Then my father spoke to me, and said, "We have a little journey to make, son."

I don't know how I got to the place, but soon I

was in a very large room, not unlike a library. The room was well lit and there were people standing in the doorway. I recognised people I knew, and family members I had not seen since my childhood. I was greeted with such love and happiness.

Then Mother said to me, "Son, let us now go and meet your guides, who, behind the scenes, were so much a part of your earthly life."

I was led to a long table where four people sat. One I seemed to recognise, but I couldn't quite place him. This gentleman stood up and shook my hand. "Hello, my boy," he said. "Life begins anew. I was your helper in your earthly life. These gentlemen were your helpers, too. And we can say it was a pleasure to walk through life with you. Go and join your family and friends now, and at some time we'll all meet again to discuss your past and your future."

I was so excited at seeing everyone that the impact of his words completely passed me by.

Joseph: You said that on earth you had a simple faith. Has that changed in any way for you in the years you have been in your special life?

Mr Watts: In many ways it is the same – I view things as I did on earth, and my beliefs are the same, but I now have a greater insight into the way life is woven together to unite both our worlds.

Joseph: I envy you to be able to have such a clear view of life in both worlds. For me it seems the more questions I ask, the more I get tangled up in the complicated answers I receive. Then to try and make sense of these answers, I seem to have to ask more complicated questions.

Mr Watts: Now you see how difficult it was for me to be a teacher to you little scallywags!

Mr Watts beamed his heart-melting smile. I felt as snug as I did as a child when he would tell us boys about pirates and treasure, which we all believed was his secret life on the high seas.

Joseph: There is a question I have asked many, many different people over the years, and you know, every answer I get is different. May I ask you, too, my dear friend?

Mr Watts: Of course you may.

Joseph: Have you met *Jesus*, and have you in some way met *God*, or are you aware of him being there? Please let me explain why I ask you such a question.

As you know, in my world it has been considered irreligious to the point of sacrilege to ask this kind of question. I well remember how doing so in my youth met with the condemnation of church leaders.

They said we are unworthy to see or speak of God in such a way, because his omnipotence is too great for us measly mortals. Yet to me, God is our father, and I'm sure he would value our asking about him. I have found him to be wonderfully communicative to his children, throughout the human experience.

But like many who have gone before me, and just as many who will come after me, I have learned that God communicates not necessarily in the way we would want him to, but in the way that we need for our understanding. Sorry I've gone around the houses to make my point.

Mr Watts: We are all aware of the presence of the Master, and also of the other great teaching souls.

One of my favourite things here is to go to the talks by the great speakers. Through their words and truth, they convey the Master's message. They communicate the reality of God's creation to us all.

It doesn't matter if there are great intellectuals or people of simple understanding at these talks – everyone understands, and everyone knows these are the words of the Master. And we are always left with a great feeling of God's love, and with hope for all creation.

There is no need to actually see the Master or any

other great soul to satisfy the premise that "seeing is believing". We already have a great sense of knowing they are here. Joseph, I would not wish in any way to see God face-to-face, because that would scar my soul with the terrible knowledge that the end of my life was nigh. No one, not even Jesus, sees God.

Joseph: Please may I ask if you are aware of, shall I say, shadowy souls?

Mr Watts: You are well aware that in your world and mine, there are souls who are ever ready to cause strife.

I make my choices when it comes to who I wish to cultivate a friendship with, just as you do. But in fairness to you, I have to say I am luckier in this world than you are in yours. It is easier for me to avoid relationships that may be damaging, because here I am aware of people's motives – something that may be missed in your world.

Joseph: You are full of wisdom, and still my mentor. Thank you for your guidance.

Would you mind if I asked you, my friend, how you think I am doing so far in this life?

Mr Watts: I will tell you with my teacher's head on. "Tries hard, could do better." On occasion you are self-centred; your guide tells me there are times when you should listen more to what is actually being said to you, rather than to your own interpretation of what is being said.

Joseph: I thought I was a good listener... If I do make wrong interpretations my guide jumps on me from a great height and corrects me.

Mr Watts: I am being told that in your dealings with people when Spirit are present you are fine, but in personal conversations you tend to make your own assumptions and interpretations, and with the best of intentions you can appear to be a bit of a know-all.

Joseph: Yes, I know what you mean. As you have said, I must try harder.

Can I remind you of something you did for me while I was at boarding school? You did many kind things for me, but this is something I'll never forget. You got a jacket for me which you'd paid for out of your own pocket. Yes, it was three times too big, but you said I would grow into it. I was made to feel the same as the other boys. Thank you, my dear friend!

My tears came back.

Mr Watts: I have enjoyed our time together, Joseph. I am well aware you would have me stay, but there are others waiting to speak with you. But we will stay in contact, and as always, you have my love. My final teacher's report to you is: "A soft-centred boy, but don't change."

Mr Watts is the only person in my life who can still make me blubber like a child.

My Birth Father Speaks His Truth

This chapter is quite painful for me, because Father left the family when I was very young. Although I met him once I had become an adult, I grew up with only my mother's version of their life together to go by. I am afraid of what he will say now, and I already feel defensive of my mother. Still, I will try my hardest to be as fair as possible.

Father: Hello Poo. I'm so happy to speak to you! I've waited so long for this moment.

Joseph: Hello, Father. Where does this "Poo" name come from?

Father: When you were a little boy you were forever filling your trousers, no matter where you were.

Mother did later confirm that this had been Father's name for me. Even so, I have to say that for his first visit to me, and at my age, surely he could have thought of a slightly more becoming way of greeting me, that would have been more helpful in calming my unease.

Father: I'm happy to say that, in my time here, I've been able to further my education, and I have been enrolled in the school that teaches all about monastic life.

Excuse me while I pick my jaw up from off the floor. This is unreal. It can only be a joke.

Father: I am hoping that sometime in the future, if I am allowed to reincarnate, I will have the chance to lead a monastic life.

Joseph: Well, Father, this is not the meeting I expected from you. But I can honestly say I'm intrigued at the turnaround from your earthly life.

Father: I realised my mistakes, and like every other soul, I wish to make amends for the mistakes I made. I was always a believer, even if I didn't put what I believed into practice. I was a psychic, up to a point.

Joseph: Mother said you read the coals in the fire.

Father: Yes, I did.

Joseph: May I ask a personal question, please. How do you see God?

Father: Being on this side for so long has given me a great insight into personal development – what it means for my own future and for other people's futures too. I think that, more than anything, personal development means understanding. And a big part of that is realising that, as a child of God, I must interact on every level that I am capable of. I was lucky to meet up with my grandfather, who I adored. He has helped me so much.

Joseph: With respect, Father, I am finding this meeting too much to take. All the time you are talking this way – and I know that from your point of view you are being honest – I keep having images of my mother's tears, and the hard life that she and my brothers and sisters have had because of your lack of caring. I was too young to share in their tears, but I know their strong feelings of distaste.

Father: I may appear insensitive to you, but while I have been here I have tried to help in every way I can. I have been and still am very aware of my misdeeds.

Joseph: Father, I am so sorry that I dared chastise you. You have come to speak to me, and in common with all souls, you should be accorded unconditional love. Because of my own feelings, I did not give you the dignity that your request to speak your truth deserves.

Father: You're a chip off the old block! You are my son, and I do want us to work together on healing the wounds I caused.

I don't wish to bore you with further conversations between my father and me, suffice it to say I am now on a much more stable footing with him.

Indri's Questions

Indri: Good evening to you. It's very nice to be here.

Joseph: Thank you for coming! It's always a delight to speak to people from the divine world. I have been told you have travelled far and wide, and observed every kind of phenomenon from levitation to trance to healing.

Indri: That's right! But something I find just as fascinating is to observe people like yourself who work with our world. I would be grateful if you would answer some questions for me.

Joseph: I will be happy to help in any way I can.

Indri: May I ask why you were chosen to do the work you do?

Joseph: Wow, that's a tough one. I have asked myself that question all my life. With respect, Indri, would it not be better to ask my guides? Although, come to think of it, they would probably be scratching their heads too..!

Indri: I have asked them many times, and other people too. It's an important question for my thesis, and no one has ever given me an answer.

Joseph: Perhaps they're genuinely baffled! I'm joking, of course. They were probably thinking that it is very important to protect people's privacy – just as it is in my world.

In all honesty, Indri, I often ask, "Why me?" And I can tell you, it's the same for other people who do this kind of work – we're all confused as to why it's us doing the job!

Let me explain what it was like for me when I was younger. I was born into an ordinary and in many ways dysfunctional family. My immediate family was not at all religious, nor were they spiritual in any sense, as far as I can tell. Until I was four years old, I was not aware of any world beyond this one. I knew nothing apart from my family, house, and friends.

My awareness of a strange world was not a blessing at the age of four. In fact it was a big pain in the rear. Please excuse my crudeness, but at least I am using a toned-down version of how it felt at the time. All the strange things I was seeing and hearing caused me no end of trouble. People would avoid me; mothers would not let their children play with me.

I did not wish for this work, Indri, and that certainly begs the question "why me?" And when I talk to other people who do the same kind of work, and ask them why they were chosen, they always have the same blank look on their faces that I do when I am asked, and they give the same answer as me: they don't know.

There is a theory that for some reason, a part of the brain can kick in on another level (I always say my mother dropped me on my head at birth), and that this somehow links into a perception that is different from how normal brain patterns work. There may be some truth in this, because even as a child I tended to think very laterally.

Another theory among people I have worked with over the years is that it is in some way a karmic experience. I am not too sure I subscribe to that theory, because it brings in all sorts of complicated moral, ethical and spiritual ramifications.

I have also asked my guides why me, but they never say. Maybe it would make me egotistical if I imagined I was special in some way.

I can only advise, Indri, that when you have a project to do as a student on the divine side of life, you find out as many facts as you can, then follow through with your own ideas and interpretations.

Indri: Thank you, Joseph. I will do that.

Joseph: May I also suggest, from my own experience, that when you are asking a question that touches on people's personal lives, you open out the theme and make it wider. This way it is clear that you are asking on a subject matter level, rather than on a personal level. I can tell you, I have worked for many years with my guides, and they are definitely very reluctant to talk about themselves. And sometimes discussing personal lives can be less straightforward than it may seem. For instance, Spirit may say something of a personal nature to me; two years down the line I will likely have forgotten many of their words of explanation. When I remember their words out of context, I may end up changing the whole meaning of what they were saying to me. We all do it; I do it when I talk about the personal qualities of my guides. Because I am so proud of them, not only do I make them out to be knights in shining armour, but I give them crowns as well. From my point of view this is perfectly true, but sometimes the way I see them does not concur with what they have actually said to me about themselves.

Truth is paramount in your world, as it should be in mine. That is why it is so good for me to speak with people on the divine side of life; there are spirits there who correct my interpretations.

Indri: May I ask how you see your role in the work you do?

Joseph: Wow, that's another good question; it has really thrown me. Please give me a minute to ask Chou for some help on this one. I have my own version about myself, but I think I could end up giving you some very theatrical answers.

Chou has arrived.

Joseph: I shall be as honest as I can. Chou will make sure I don't put on top and tails and dance across the Albert Hall of my imagination. Here I go:

When I was young and special things were happening in my life – things from the spirit world – it was like having a new train set, to tell the truth. I wanted to play all the time. The learning part was a drag – I wasn't keen on that at all. But seeing and hearing the different Spirit in their shining clothes, and all the magical things I was shown – that was what I really liked. Not being from a refined background where one is taught to act serenely, I was very upfront, and with the benefit of hindsight, I think it is fair to say I was very crass. Over the years I have mellowed, and hopefully got things in proportion.

If I am to put my hand on my heart, I have to say that, in my early days, I thought I was something a bit special. This coloured my approach to life, but the big "I am" didn't last long, for I had a Titus guiding me. Titus taught me that I was very lucky to wipe the feet of Life. And since then, the years have taught me how lucky I am to work for Spirit.

To me, working with the spirit world is like being an explorer – finding new territories to cross and spectacular landscapes for my world to see – all the time being pushed forward towards new wonders and constant innovations. Every time I find a new land of knowledge to explore, I get so excited!

I am part of a team. I am in this world but my bosses are in the next; I am the one who taps the keys.

Thank heavens for computers! I take my hat off to all those writers from days gone by, who had to copy everything out by hand.

And so my work has progressed. I am in awe of my teachers, like us all when we are learning a new skill. As I have got older, I have wanted to learn, and now I find it a joy. Of course, as you listen to teachers that you admire, their teaching rubs off on you, often on levels you are not aware of in your everyday life. But it is there when you need it.

On a spiritual level, I often feel I take two steps forward and six steps back. That's me – I confuse myself, by being too analytical. Sometimes what is said to me may be as it is, but no, I go and ruin it by trying to be clever, and I end up being the proverbial pain.

You never see yourself as others see you. You would think I would know better about things, working with Spirit. But I still get frustrated. Other people see me as that nice man with a kind smile, but inside I am a mass of worries about whether I am up to the job.

Do you know, Indri, what concerns me most about my work? It's that I am dealing with people every day of my life. I must get it right. I am working for Spirit, so there is no room for mistakes. What I say and do on behalf of Spirit affects people's lives for years to come, perhaps all their lives. The feedback I get – from all sorts of people – is magical, yet I still doubt whether I have done enough.

I see my work, especially my books, as passing

something on to people; a different way of looking at matters of the inner self, for instance.

I still love the church and its wonderful ministers, and I love other faiths and their ideals. Occasionally people put me in a box labelled "Spiritualist". I'm sorry, but there's no way that is me.

The truth is, I follow no religion. Religions cause wars, but faith saves souls. I have a faith in God.

My work is to listen to those who know best, and to learn.

Sorry, I have gone on a bit, Indri; Chou tells me that I can chops for Britain. As you will have noticed, I have been trying to justify myself by explaining how I feel, rather than really focusing on Spirit and my commitment to what we need to achieve. I am actually not one hundred percent sure how I should be seeing the work I do with Spirit. What I think would be helpful to you would be for me to ask someone completely different to come and talk to you (well… to both of us, actually!) to explain why things work the way they do.

Indri: Thank you Joseph, for your time, and for your informative talk. I hope you don't mind me saying I am little the wiser about your work with Spirit. God bless you.

Joseph: I can only agree with you, Indri, that is why I will ask someone who knows about these things to come and talk to us.

Malakai Speaks His Knowledge

Malakai: Hello, Joseph. I'm pleased to see you. I understand you would like to learn more about how my world works, and why the system is the way it is.

Joseph: Welcome, Malakai. Yes! There are some things I have tried to get my mind around, and failed. I am very grateful to you for coming to talk to me.

Malakai: You're very welcome. Please ask your questions.

Joseph: I should start by telling you that over the years I have asked a lot of questions to many, many souls, and they have given wonderful answers, but I'm still always intrigued to hear other people's explanations and points of view. Please bear with me if some of my questions sound basic and naïve.

Before I start asking Malakai the questions I've got prepared here, it occurs to me that I have another,

different question. Well, it is not so much a question –
more a wondering on my part, and on the part of
*the whole world. I am fascinated to know where **God***
came from. If I knew that, I would be the second most
famous person in history! Ha ha!

Joseph: In the beginning, when God made heaven,
do you think he created all souls at the same time, or
was it a gradual process?

Malakai: It is logical to me that the Creator made
some souls sooner and others later, according to his
wisdom. As you know with the Creator, absolutely
everything is done for a reason that is totally divine,
and with a seeing and a knowing that go far beyond
the comprehension either of humans or Spirit.

The soul is a living, thinking energy that no
power can destroy. Souls were blessed with wisdom,
in greater or lesser degrees, which fitted the Creator's
thinking. Originally heaven was created for the
power of spiritkind, and for their interaction. But as
time passed – on a scale which human beings cannot
conceive of – a system that had been designed by
the Supreme Deity was evolving in all its glory. This
system was to be a perfect creation. It was made up
of different souls, each with their own individual
ideals, and it involved a sharing of power.

Over a period of time beyond logical contemplation, powers were granted on the individual scale. These powers were meant to complement the flourishing of God's heaven. However they eventually grew to such an extent that they became incompatible with the plan of the Creator. The Creator bore with these powers of self-will, because he had made them as individuals. He was not and is not an egotistical God. He allowed them the chance to reunite with him.

Some of these powers had decided that they knew better than the Perfect Deity how heaven should be developed. In time, these powers grew to be a challenge. As you know from elementary chemistry, when two opposing energies clash, they cause an almighty explosion. I suggest to you that this is what your scientists call the Big Bang theory. This clash, of unimaginable proportions, caused the release of all sorts of elements, which eventually manifested themselves as physical phenomena.

Joseph: What you are saying is fascinating, but I am puzzled. God is the perfect creator, so why were negative energies created in the first place, that would oppose his creation?

Malakai: I did not say they were negative energies.

Joseph: So what kind of energies were they?

Malakai: They were energies with different ways of seeing and doing things. There must always be opposites to allow for development; this gives rise to a proper order, and then to a perfect system.

Joseph: Sorry, Malakai, maybe I'm being dense here, but if opposites were created to make a perfect system, then why was there conflict?

Malakai: Opposites, yes. Not opposing forces – that's when conflict comes into play.

Joseph: Please forgive me, I promise I am not challenging you. But from the point of view of the Creator, why create something that would only end up negating your creation of perfection?

Malakai: I did not say I had all the answers, Joseph. I am giving you my considered opinion, and you would need to ask God your question.

Joseph: Sorry Malakai, I am being analytical again.

I won't be asking God that question in my prayers.

Malakai: Next question please, Joseph.

Joseph: In your opinion, does Satan exist as a power in the physical and the unseen world?

Malakai: That is a naïve question, Joseph, of course he does. Over time he has lost his purity, and has been cut off from the perfect creation. In a sense he has become a rolling stone. With nowhere to rest, he has gathered only negativity. He exists in the world of physical energy, and in the empty space of nowhere, commonly known as hell.

Whereas the Creator's energy is a positive energy – so constant both in this world and yours that it can be drawn on at all times, Satan's energy is a negative energy. It is not possible for this negative energy to be constant. There is no structure to allow it to stick to anything, tangible or intangible. Satan's power is only strong when it picks up negative thoughts, which he joins together to mould his will. It is within each individual's power to cultivate positivity. Rejecting negative thought is easy.

Thoughts are living energies with substance. They act and react in the physical universe, in the divine world, and also in the space we call hell.

Positive thoughts establish a creative energy which is like a solid substance – real and alive. Positive thoughts help you grow into anything you wish to be. They are your link to God's heaven and all the souls in God's creation.

Joseph: Thank you, Malakai.

The Story of Robert

One day my guide Chou told me he was going to bring a young man from the spirit world to me, so I could help him. I told Chou that would be fine.

"Wait and see what help he wants, first," replied Chou.

To cut a long story short, ten days later Chou appeared with Robert. Byron, my one-eared cat, was the first to see them. He came flying into the kitchen, with his one ear flat to his head. He jumped up on the table and gave me a cat's mouthful of anger, and a look as if to say, "Your mates are here again, and I'm not happy about giving up my chair!" I went into the living room where I saw Chou and Robert sitting on the sofa – but here I must explain something to you.

I say that I saw Robert; what I really saw was

Robert as if I were looking at him through cheese-cloth. Chou saw my look of surprise. He explained that Robert was not happy at meeting a human being again so soon after leaving the physical world.

Robert began, in a very emotional way, to tell his story. The big softie in me made its way to the fore – I started to well up with tears – but I had to appear strong for this young man. I was advised by Chou to keep some details about Robert's situation private. This is to protect Robert and other people who are still living here in this world.

When he was on earth, Robert lived in Norfolk. He was born to a single mother in the early 1970s. Her circumstances were such that Robert had to be fostered out to a relative in the first eighteen months of his life. But the relative became sick, so Robert went into care. From there – as far as I can ascertain – he was adopted, although not legally. I feel sure from listening to the conversation as we went along that some kind of deal was done on a private level.

The result of all this was that Robert ended up living only seven miles from his birth mother. When he was about thirteen, Robert became aware of his adoption, and of where his birth mother lived. That was when he went off the rails. In society's terms, he became a "problem child" and for about two years he was uncontrollable. At this point, I must leave out many personal details.

He ran away to Liverpool – well, at least that's where he found himself. Needing to survive, and trying to deal with his problems, he went into drugs, and stole to live. He got into other nefarious situations, all the time sinking deeper into a mire of self-destruction. By the time he was seventeen he was selling drugs as well as taking them. This got totally out of hand. Sad to say he overdosed, and the inevitable happened.

I have given you as many details as I can about Robert. But for Robert to be able to move on, he needed to let out all his emotions, from all the terrible times he had been through. I heard everything about him.

I was so moved by his story that I was deeply upset for weeks afterwards. Somehow within myself I could not come to terms with what had happened to him.

But that was not the end of the story. Robert had asked me to go and see his birth mother and his adopted parents. I knew I had to do it, but I spent weeks with terrible mixed feelings. I wanted to do right by Robert, but I'm sure you can imagine how uncomfortable I felt. What do you say to parents in circumstances like these? I was a total stranger. Where would I say I got this information from? I didn't know the people's personal circumstances. Was I to say, "I have spoken to your son from beyond the grave, and…" If someone came up to me and said something like that, I might feel like saying "B***** off, you nutcase" myself. But the worst thing of all for me was, were they aware that Robert had died?

So off I went on this sad journey to Norfolk. By the time I reached the house of his adoptive parents, I was one mass of confusion. I didn't know how I was going to introduce myself, let alone start a conversation. And it was very little help to me that Chou kept saying everything would be all right. I was so uptight that if I had been given the Holy Grail to drink from, I still would have been a gibbering wreck.

I knocked on the door, and it was opened by a lady in her mid-forties. In my haste and desperation I just blurted out who I was and why I had come. She looked at me for a few moments, then smiled, and said, "Come in." Thank heavens, I thought. I went into the sitting room. In an armchair sat a man who, without knowing who I was, got up to shake my hand.

The lady told him who I was and why I had come. He smiled and sat down. In fact they were both all smiles. The lady went to put the kettle on. Thank heavens, I thought, for the second time. But by now I was feeling uneasy for a different reason. I was a total stranger. Why were they just accepting me there in their home so unquestioningly?

Tea arrived. I jumped straight in and said what I had come to say, and passed on the personal information that Robert had wanted me to convey.

There were tears from them. And there were tears from me, too. Partly because I was so happy for them, and partly because I could feel all those weeks of tension inside me easing away.

Then this kind lady said to me, "We knew all about Robert's life and his death. What you have told us today, no one else knew about – only Robert and us. I have asked God a dozen times a day to please send us help, so we can try to understand why Robert did what he did."

I am skipping over a lot of details here, but after a time, I asked if it would be possible to speak to Robert's birth mother. "Yes, of course," the lady told me. And so I met his birth mother. She was a lovely lady, too, and we spent a long time talking together.

Here I would like to make a personal observation. It is not a criticism of anyone, or the circumstances they may find themselves in. But I do feel that it is better to tell children when they are young that they are adopted (once again, depending on the circumstances) rather than waiting until they are older when nature kicks in and they are very vulnerable to their emotions.

Over the years I have talked with Robert again. What a different young man he is, from when we first met. He is now a very happy bunny.

Mary-Anne – Fun and Laughter

This little spirit girl came to speak to a group of us one evening.

Mary-Anne: Hello, everyone, my name is Mary-Anne, and I am here with Sister Maria.

Everyone at our meeting greeted Mary-Anne, and asked her to say a hello to Sister Maria too. I was chairing this meeting. (Sounds grand, doesn't it?)

Joseph: It's very kind of you to visit our little meeting, Mary-Anne. May I say what a lovely name you have.

Mary-Anne: Thank you. I'm here because I came top of my class at drawing.

Everyone claps, and there are smiles all around. This is normal procedure in these circumstances, when children come for an accolade they have earned.

Mary-Anne: I'm writing a story about God.

More claps and smiles.

Mary-Anne: I'm going to write a funny story about God, so can you all help me, please?

David, a member of our group, is wonderfully irreverent, in a gentle way.

David: OK, my little darling, let's see. How about writing about God going to a party dressed as Father Christmas?

Mary-Anne: That's a silly idea.

I know this seems disrespectful and I hope I don't offend anyone, but the idea of God in another role appeared to have sparked off the ridiculous in us all.

Here are some of the suggestions that came out of our silliness: God as a funny magician with a tickling stick. God as Willy Wonka (of chocolate factory fame) raining down sweets as a treat. And God as the chief taxman, saying, "No more tax for anyone!" (I think that was my favourite one.)

Luckily we did manage to come up with one that Mary-Anne really liked, which was God as a magical king, with a magic wand that sparkled when he granted wishes. We had to dress God in all the clothes of a magical king to set the scene.

After a time Mary-Anne and Sister Maria left. Goodness knows what Sister Maria had thought of us –

she had every right to think we were a bunch of soggy biscuits. To tell the truth, when prayer time came to end the meeting, we were all a bit contrite, in case we had overstepped the mark. I'm happy to say there was no comeback, so I assume all was well.

Blue Brother James
Speaks with Authority

For some considerable time now, I have been asking to speak with someone about how God and the divine world see the development of the human race. Five years after I first made my request, it was answered:

James: I have come this evening in answer to your request to learn our views on certain matters.

Joseph: Welcome! It is a joy to receive you in my home. And I am so happy my request has been answered!

James: Shall we begin?

Joseph: Of course.

Could you please tell me if you think we are more spiritually advanced on earth now than the people who lived in biblical times?

James: I would ask you to ask questions that are answerable in the time you have.

To answer one part of your question – and this is the simplified answer to it – I can tell you that spirituality is in the doing. In a way, you are more advanced now spiritually, inasmuch as nations are more aware of their people's needs. This "national" spirituality has come about out of the needs of the people, but more in the sense that governments are aware that without certain needs of the people being met, the governments' own welfare would be compromised. Nevertheless, in this way, national identities have been formed, and this has brought about a certain kind of security for nations. When basic needs are met, certain bonds are formed, then other needs come into play.

Within this structure the churches have played their part. For a long time they cracked the spiritual whip, planting the fear that a soul was in mortal danger if it did not conform to certain edicts. Often these edicts were transcribed selectively from holy scriptures to suit the way people in positions of power wished the national identity to develop. Each society sees its national power in a particular way, and then accordingly, that is the way that spirituality is seen.

Within the national belief there are also organised

systems of beliefs – faiths both old and new. And then within these faiths, or very often completely independently of them, there is people's personal spirituality, played out on a day-to-day basis. This binds people together, and it is usually what helps a society most. The beliefs that go to make up a person's spirituality are the working weave of life. Normally they are kept within the heart and soul of a person. Such people carry out sterling deeds on the basis of their personal trust in God – much like in the early times when the cosmos was forming and there was a need to have an inner belief in a God, rather than in a people. So on these levels you have moved forward.

But people in centuries past had more of a trust in God. In the early days of the world, most people did not have their basic needs met by a stable society, so their personal trust in a God was paramount.

This is a simplified view, of course, because as you know, while all this was going on, there have been people attempting to reach God in the most diverse ways imaginable. Some have been cruel on a national scale; others have imposed regimes of fear onto societies, out of their misguided beliefs.

Spirituality usually survives in its true form in

a person's heart and soul, and it evolves through a person's experience of life. A person's belief in God the creator, with his pure, unconditional love, brings hope. This applies equally to all people, irrespective of creeds or cultures.

It is fraught with danger for people to put their spiritual trust in mankind, because each faith teaches its own code of belief.

People reach out to God from their inner being in order to experience a oneness with him. This is usually by their deeds and the way they lead their lives.

One-to-one prayer gives reassurance that you are identified with the Creator in your own way. Collective prayer gives reassurance on a community level, and states to the world that you are strong in faith.

Faiths and beliefs change with the passing of time, for one reason or another. Within this changing there is always strong spirituality, and there has always been personal spirituality, so I believe that over time, the human experience of spirituality is ever the same.

Joseph: Is part of what you are saying – and stop me if I am wrong – that if faiths and religions are truly believed in, then they are right? Surely there can be only one truth.

James: Throughout human history there have been great spiritual masters blessed with great spiritual minds. Each one has had a part to play in developing spirituality on all levels. The essence of what every great master teaches is the same, no matter what his people's social condition may be. God's truth is the same in any language or belief. Every religion is built on its own great teachers, and the teachers are all cut from the same cloth.

Where religions become corrupt is in their interpretation, which is usually carried out by lesser minds. Either these lesser minds have another agenda they wish to follow, or they wish to create an identity for their own people that states that righteousness is theirs, that they are the one link with God, and they must therefore be the chosen people. Look at your history. Every nation has tried, at some time, to impose its own will on another nation. Power is the key here. Words are inserted, for whatever purpose. Usually it is to say: "We are right and you are wrong."

No great master ever taught this. The great masters often taught within the bounds of a culture's understanding, but the themes of all the masters are the same. As the saying goes, all roads lead to Rome. For the purposes of our talk right now, that means all roads lead to *God*.

Joseph: But I truly believe that Jesus Christ was the Son of God, and God's heart and eyes on earth. While I love to hear and read of the other great masters that have been on Earth, and I have learned a lot from their teaching, Christianity teaches us that Jesus Christ was the Son of God. The Master himself said, "I am the Shepherd", and "I am the Way, the Truth and the Life. No one comes to the Father but by me."

James: As I have said, there are many roads to God. The Son of God is from the Godhead – the ultimate son of Man. In Christ, God came in person, as a teacher. The highest came amid the lowest. This shows God's love for humankind.

Joseph: I agree with you, of course, but in my world, other faiths would see your statement as meaning that their great teachers were in a lesser role, and were therefore lesser in their awareness of truth. This worries me and hurts me for them.

James: You have taken my statement and interpreted it according to your way of thinking, Joseph. You have done this out of just thinking for others,

I might add. But it does prove my point about interpretation.

What I have said to you is this: All the great
teachers and masters are cut from the same cloth.
They originate from the heart and the eyes of God.
They sit at the same hand of God as Jesus does. All the
great masters have humility, but they do not play the
game of false modesty. They are true beings of light
and knowledge. They are beyond being bothered
about names and titles – they leave that kind of thing
to Man.

Joseph: I have great love and respect for the
Buddha and his teachings, I also have great love for
Mohammed and his teachings, and I have an all-
enveloping love of Jesus and his teachings. Can I
then, in my heart, follow all three teachings? Would
I, in a way, be serving three masters?

James: Have you not heard anything I have said to
you, Joseph? I have already told you that the essence
of what every great master teaches is the same, and
that all the great teachers are cut from the same cloth.
They reach out to people through their divinity, and
with their own personalities. But the cloth is the
same. The truths that they voice reach many millions
of different people, who interpret them in a way that

touches them personally. So the truth can come from many voices. Your truth comes from your belief in the Son of Man.

Joseph: Thank you, James. That is much clearer to me now. I needed to understand that all truths are the same when it comes to teaching God's law. It is in the interpretation that I must allow some flexibility.

James: It is the flexibility of an open heart that can bring true spirituality.

Next question, please.

Joseph: I have hundreds of questions to ask you, but we would both be here until we grew old. But if I could just ask you one thing… Could you please tell me what life in the spirit world is like for you personally? I am well aware of the fun and humour – my own guide is living proof of that – but could you explain what a typical day is like for you?

James: There is no such thing as a typical day in the sense that you mean, because our lives are not ordered by time. My job is to work together with my brothers and sisters to help souls here to develop their spirituality, and to improve your lives in the physical world. I have been doing this for a long time, and it is always a great joy to me.

I start my "day" with meetings, petitions, and talks

with all kinds of people. We are lucky in that we can store vast amounts of knowledge in microseconds, and draw upon it just as quickly – pretty much like your computers. We are not table-and-chair people; we are foot-and-movement people.

Meaning that they do not sit at desks all day, but are out and about.

I went on to ask James if he would mind talking about himself as a person. It would be nice to feel we were two friends chatting about our day's work over a cup of tea (a presumption on my part) because I would like to understand better where James is coming from.

James: One of my favourite things is to visit the halls of souls who are about to reincarnate.

Joseph: Wow, James! You have hit on one of my favourite subjects! When my time comes to leave this world, I would love to train to be an adviser in the halls of reincarnation.

Would you be able to tell me a little bit about the process of reincarnation, and why we reincarnate?

Sorry, James, carry on.

James: I love seeing the joy and feeling the excitement when souls are about to leave, congratulating them and wishing them luck.

Another part of my work is to receive returning

souls, and to work with souls who have returned in difficult circumstances. Some souls return here as a result of war, some pass over in circumstances where there has been mass death, and some return suddenly and unexpectedly.

Joseph: I am shuddering… It sounds like a very heavy commitment, James.

James: The key to fulfilling this commitment is unconditional love. It takes a lot of experience, too.

Another part of the work of the blue brothers and blue sisters is to carry out God's instructions as delivered by his angels.

It fills me with joy to think of majestic and magical angels delivering God's instructions for the worlds both seen and unseen. I feel as excited as a little boy.

James: Another thing I love doing when I have finished my work is to go to a service with my family and friends. It is always a thrill for me to see people giving of themselves for the glory of God. It is not as you would imagine it on Earth. There are all kinds of performers and events. There are bands, heavenly choirs, and talks on every conceivable subject and at every level. Some of the talks are given by angels and archangels, others are given by children. And there are comedians and jesters – they are great fun.

Joseph: Can anyone go to these services? If they can, there must be an amazing sound system…

James: Yes, we are all God's children. There is no elitism here, although of course there are souls who have reached their divinity. There are no different categories of seating to separate the people; you will find all the kingdom of heaven sitting together, enjoying the service and celebrating the glory of God.

Joseph: I feel so envious, James, but I can feel your excitement. I shall look forward to this pleasure one day! Happy times to come!

James: It is time I went – I still have work to finish. But it has been a great joy for me to talk with you. I'm sorry I wasn't able to answer all your questions this time. We will meet again. God's blessings on you.

Joseph: Thank you, James. Please excuse the tear in my eye. I can't express the happiness I feel right now. It has been a magical time for me.

Be Aware, Be Safe and Be Happy

In reality, everyone who wishes to develop an awareness of the divine world can do so. I assure you it is not necessarily those who may be seen as mighty or good who achieve this awareness, but everyday souls who live their lives according to their lot. I have often wondered how many people miss out on the marvellous experience in life of speaking with their guides because of prejudice from the world.

If you have an interest in this field, you should, as is the case with many things in life, start off by doing some research. Read books, talk to people, enquire at the churches.

After some serious thought, and plenty of talking to the right people, you may decide you would like to go and see a person who works with the divine world. There is no doubt that there are people in this line of work who are so genuinely good that you are left with a deep sense of humility. But you must ensure that the person you choose to consult is one you have made extensive enquiries about. People who are genuine will have no objections to your doing this. On the contrary, they will be glad to know that you insist on verifying the quality of their work. Do not be afraid of seeking the divine world – it is your right. But ensure you take all the precautions you need to.

Please do **not** go to séances. Séances can be very dangerous, unless they are run by people who are very experienced and very competent. The rule of thumb is: don't go, and the only exception would be when a séance is run by a registered, experienced and trusted member of a Spiritualist church.

Please do **not** use ouija boards. They can be very dangerous.

Checklist

1) Sort out clearly in your mind the reason why you wish to reach into the divine world; in order to do this properly, you may have to bide your time for a while. Remember, you do not have to have a

religious reason. Your reason may be one of personal importance to you.

2) Always make sure you go to a person whom you know to be of true conscience regarding the divine world. This may sometimes be a minister of one of the established churches. It may also be a minister or other member of one of the Spiritualist churches. But check locally first to see that they are registered, and not some offshoot of a weird sect.

Any person worth their salt who works with the divine world will be happy to speak to you about their work, and would never take you beyond where you wish to go.

3) Never, ever go to someone who charges enormous amounts of money. I say "Fake!" and I would happily say that to their faces.

4) People who ask for money up front are a no-no in our work.

5) Please also remember that people have to live; many people spend their lives doing this very valuable work and they also wish to have a quality of life, so expect to pay something.

6) If you should decide to go to a church, never, ever pay a fee. It would be wicked to do so, and no soul in the divine world would wish you to. You are

in God's house, and he charges you nothing for help. (You are of course welcome to make a donation in line with what you consider that you can afford.) The exception to this rule is when a church hosts a meeting given by a visiting speaker who may have had to travel a great distance, and stay over for however long the meeting or series of meetings runs for. In any case, you will generally find that these churches are run by honest, dedicated and wonderfully loyal people, who will give you a warm welcome.

7) Avoid people who ask you questions. Remember it will be obvious that you are there to find out something. Never volunteer information. Be responsive if you find there is something you can relate to, but do not go over the top and give anything away.

8) If you visit a medium or a seer, there is never any need for you to sit in a darkened place.

9) Remember the golden rule that you must **never, ever** join anything that you do not feel happy with. Go by your instincts, and do not be afraid to ask questions.

10) Do not go to see anyone just so that you can talk to a loved one who has passed on. We cannot command people to come and speak to you. What we can do is tell you about how the divine world can

help you. I know how difficult it is to reach out and hope when we have lost a loved one. But please accept this advice from someone who has worked in this field for very many years.

11) Remember, God answers prayers – people do not. People can help you and advise you, but your spiritual development is between God and you. Remember this, and you will not go far wrong.

Be aware, be safe and be happy.

Meditation

I find that meditation is the easiest way to reach the divine world. There are hundreds of different ways of meditating, but this is what I do:

First I sit down and have a cup of tea. I make sure I am warm, and as completely comfortable and relaxed as possible. Then I sing one of my favourite songs or hymns. (It's a wonder that this puts me into a relaxed state, because I can't sing a note in tune.) I say the Lord's Prayer, then I settle to what I call *daydreaming.* In my mind, I imagine I am healing the sick, and travelling to far-off lands to feed the hungry. All this lifts me from my everyday thoughts, and sets the stage for me to drift into deep meditation.

So try this for a while, until you feel happy and comfortable with it. Remember, your aim is to speak to God in a happy and relaxed state, to really put your trust in him, and to let him speak to you when you are ready. And *God will*, because in him you can trust.

I make no apology for saying that when I am dealing with a matter of great importance, I choose God as the expert. I do not go to human experts – not even those with a lifetime's experience. When a person has a matter of deep concern and I ask the divine world a question on their behalf, I am always given an answer that is a practical application of the teachings of God, presented with both depth and simplicity. I have never yet found the same quality of answer to originate from the earthly side of life.

Prayer

Please remember this very important point: it is not always the way of God that you will make contact with the divine world in the way I do. God may choose you to be one of his very special children, and ask you to use the power of prayer.

The power of love and the power of prayer are

the greatest energies we have in the universe. God entrusts these to you, and this, in turn, is what makes you so powerful. It is in light of this that I wrote earlier in this chapter that you should question why you want to make contact with the divine world. God's love is unconditional. God calls and we must listen.

Individuality and Service

With genuine humility I thank all the kind souls who have helped me write this book and the other books I am credited with. Transcribing conversations with the spirit world was the easy part; but holding on to the knowledge I have gained has proved much more difficult, as I was damaged by the doctrines of my church and of the society I grew up in, with their narrow and limiting views of the world.

I cannot express how grateful I am that, by the grace of God, I have been able to gain a true and honest knowledge of God, and the souls in his creation on both sides of life. The unconditional love that I have been shown by the divine world has allowed me to grow, to understand that all God's creation is built on love, to put aside the prejudices that exist between different peoples and religions, and to accept that every individual has the right to their own opinion.

Every single person, both in this world and the next, is an individual. We are all different, with different needs in every way: spiritually and physically, to name but two. Even among children born to the same parents, you will find from day one that each child has his or her own personal likes and dislikes, needs, and way of thinking. So it follows that different people will take different approaches as they work towards developing their souls. We all need to be able to learn things so that we can advance in our lives. But it is our inner selves that must experience inner knowing. Then we can determine what is right for each one of us as an individual.

If we seem to be out of step with the laws and customs of the society we live in, we may need to look at ourselves and work out why we are at odds with our fellow human beings. But if our inner self is out of step with one or other of the religions as they are practised in our society, then we may very well wish to question not only ourselves but the religion too. In other words, we should first discern our own spirit, and then confidently reach out to become who we really are in the eyes of our Creator.

In the Bible, the Koran, and indeed all the magnificent books of faith and development, the great gifted souls all state, in their varying ways, that we are here not just to serve ourselves, but to serve others too, and life itself.

Every single soul that is born on Earth, without exception, has some kind of gift that it can use to help it in its own development, or to serve mankind with, or both. And each one of us has a responsibility to another person or to other people – whether we may be expressing the gifts of helping and caring in their many forms, or of artistic ability, or of scientific progress, or indeed any of the thousands of other gifts that go to make up the human experience. Those of us who have the special gift of ruling over people have a greater responsibility, and consequently a greater answerability to God, for the Creator and Supreme Ruler demands the highest of integrity.

Don't get anxious about God. Don't get anxious about religions, and don't get yourself embroiled in doctrines that are repressive and limiting to your soul. Live by the grace of God; that is a very simple way to live. Do not do as others would do; instead do as Christ or the other great spiritual masters would do. Follow the simple philosophy of their teachings.

It is your right to live life to the full as God intended you to, and to develop all your potential.

My Personal View of God

My view of God is very different from many established perceptions of him. I believe God to be a joyous God, who is full of fun and laughter. From what souls in the divine world tell me about him, he has a great sense of humour.

When I pray to him, I never, ever feel the need to be on bended knee or to go all pious; instead I speak with him in a natural way. I speak to him in the way he knows I speak as a person. I speak words naturally and from my heart – not in the stylised way of the organised religions. The only concession I make to this principle is the Lord's Prayer.

As I am a great believer in the life of Christ, I feel honoured, when I pray to God, to ask the Master to intercede for me. But there are occasions when I go straight to God. This is usually when I am in a great hurry, for example in the case of a road accident. I was once present, several years ago, as a man lay dying on the side of the road. With his eyes he was asking me for my prayers, and I had to reassure him very quickly that I was praying for him while he was leaving this world.

The way I was taught about God when I was a child, I sometimes wonder why I do not tremble in terror at his name. I was taught about God in the same way that children are sometimes told a bogey-man will come and get them if they do something naughty.

I remember how I once told a friend something my guide had said to me. My friend, in turn, mentioned what I had said to his father, who told one of my uncles. This uncle was a Bible-punching tyrant who was incapable of love or human feelings and saw nothing but holy justice in his harsh ways. It wasn't long before I was hauled before Uncle. I was ordered to stand in front of him, keep my hands behind my back, look him straight in the eye and repeat to him the wickedness I had spoken. (I can see the funny side of it now – Uncle had a huge red nose and squinty little eyes, and I was made to stand about two inches away from his face; we must both have looked ridiculous.) As instructed, I told him what I had told my friend. Uncle knocked me to the other side of the room for repeating my so-called wickedness in front of him. He seemed to have forgotten that he had ordered me to. Then he began his holy crusade, ranting at me how God would come down in the night and take my soul. He would throw me into a fire, and I would scream forever, and God would just laugh at my torment. Uncle told me all sorts of other horrid things that God would do to me, which I will not repeat here.

Poor old Uncle has been back to see me since, and a very contrite soul he is.

The minister of our church saw things very much the same way that Uncle did, telling me that God would send devils after me if I ever talked about Spirit. Strange people, these holy crusaders, I concluded. Even as a child, I knew God to be very different from the way people said he was.

The Master teaches there is a life after this life, and we must prepare for it. And from talking with souls in the divine world, I know full well that I exist after this earthly life, that all that I am survives, that I go on learning and growing spiritually, and that I do not lie dormant until a Judgement Day as this would be a total waste of God's power and love. I know that ordinary souls like myself can and do visit the Earth again in the love of God and for the good of mankind. I totally believe God's word when he says that there is no nepotism in his love and we are all equal in his sight.

When I look through the Bible, and through history itself, I am aware that those who are chosen to serve are the people who truly are aware spiritually of God's omnipotence, and who see him in the light of a father who cares and who loves his creation. But we need only look around the world to see we are still in our infancy. I sometimes feel very angered and disturbed by the princes of the church who take away the glory and magnificence of God by placing him in the role of a vengeful punisher, instead of encouraging people to see that good, positive ways pay off, and that by doing things in a natural and kind way, we are not under the stress of threats of all sorts of spiritual horrors when we leave this world.

Souls from the divine side of life have taught me how God looks upon our earthly world, and I have learned that God sees his children as we really are: children in his sight. He cares for us in the way that we care for our children – with love and careful understanding.

God gives his love unconditionally and creatively. And the history of the spiritual development of the human race proves this point. At different times through the ages, God has sent good and true spiritual leaders to show us the way; that is a sign of his love towards us. And by sending us his own son, the Master Jesus, he has given us the ultimate sign of the highest form of love. As far as I am concerned, a God who does these things for us is not going to allow us to be cast into a fiery furnace because we are ignorant of our spirituality. His punishment for us is in *bringing us into a full awareness* of everything that we, as human beings, have portrayed of ourselves towards others.

Another personal point of view is that I cannot believe a loving God would demand sacrifices as the Old Testament intimates that he does. It simply makes no sense. If this were so, why send the Master Jesus to tell us to love and respect all life? After all, Jesus cleansed the pig, he did not sacrifice it. It is indisputable that animals are a part of God's creation. God gave dominion over animals to the human race, but he also gave humans the honour of loving them and taking charge of their welfare. The Creator has no need of such symbolism from his children. Christ taught us that God only requires of us that we lead our lives in such a way as to bring ourselves into our spirituality, for this life, and for the life to come which through his son Jesus Christ we are promised.

So I can say, with hand on heart, that I believe this to be true:

Punishment is meat for the human race,
Forgiveness is the flower of God.
Sacrifice is the whip of mankind,
Love is the hope from God.

And from my knowledge of the divine world, I absolutely believe that the teachings of the Master Jesus are so very true:

Behold, I stand at the door and knock.
Knock, and the door shall be opened.
Seek, and ye shall find.
I go to prepare a place for you in my Father's kingdom.

This is true spiritual love, and true spiritual hope.